John Macquarrie

Christian Unity
and
Christian Diversity

SCM PRESS LTD

334 00176 5

First published 1975
by SCM Press Ltd
56 Bloomsbury Street London

© SCM Press Ltd 1975

Printed in Great Britain by
Richard Clay (The Chaucer Press) Ltd
Bungay, Suffolk

Christian Unity and Christian Diversity

also by John Macquarrie

The Concept of Peace
The Faith of the People of God
God-Talk
Paths in Spirituality
Principles of Christian Theology
Thinking about God
Twentieth-Century Religious Thought

To the Right Reverend
Horace William Baden Donegan
Twelfth Bishop of New York
with respect and affection

Contents

Preface

This is a book about Christian unity, but equally it is a book about Christian diversity, and the thesis is that diversity is just as essential as unity to the well-being of the Christian church. To combine unity with freedom is a very difficult task, and the temptations to uniformity are very great. But a truly Christian unity can never be a tightly knit affair. It must leave room not just for the preservation but for the continuing development of the rich heritage of different Christian traditions in which men and women of very different types have come to know the inexhaustible resources of the Christian faith. The church of the future will manifest more clearly the visible unity of the people of God and it will be a new creation, but it will also be continuous with the church of the ages and will gather up undiminished the wealth of forms which Christianity has brought forth.

Christ Church,   John Macquarrie
Oxford
October 1974

I

Unity, Diversity and Division

In early boyhood I used to be taken unwillingly on Sunday evenings to a drab little undenominational mission hall in a grey shipbuilding town on Clydeside. Inscribed in gilt letters on a red background above the rostrum were the words: *All One in Christ Jesus.* The words, of course, did not mean much to me at that time, but they must have represented some vision or aspiration among those who had founded the mission during one of the evangelistic revivals of the nineteenth century.

But, to judge from the sermons of the lay preachers who from week to week spoke in that building, the conception of oneness in Christ was very restricted. There were many polemical references to other Christian bodies. Roman Catholicism came in for special denunciation. There was a large Roman Catholic church only two streets away and many Roman Catholics in the town, but in those days there was no real communication between the Catholic and Protestant communities and they lived in mutual fear and ignorance of each other. There was also a small Scottish Episcopal church in the town, but it was always pejoratively called the 'English church' and to religious prejudice there was added in this case a confused nationalist sentiment of resentment against English ascendancy. Even the four Presbyterian churches in the town came in for criticism, for they were alleged to have diluted in various ways the purity of the gospel.

Clearly, there was a deep contradiction between the profession of unity in Christ on the one hand and lack of under-

I

standing and charity towards fellow Christians on the other. It did not arise from any conscious hypocrisy. Nor was it deliberate malice, for most of those concerned were warm humane people in their private lives, and so were most of those against whom they inveighed. No doubt there were various motives at work. Religious convictions are so central that the very existence of an alternative set of beliefs can be seen as a threat to one's own security. But this in turn implies that one's religious convictions are deeply and even passionately held. Where it has all become a matter of indifference, then one can tolerate anything and this is often the case today. What seems like the most generous broadmindedness in matters religious may be due to the fact that everything has become acceptable because nothing is actually accepted in any depth. Tolerance and generosity are easy where there is no longer any depth of conviction. But then one has only the appearance of tolerance and generosity. These qualities are really present when there are deep convictions and deep differences, and yet, in spite of them, there is a reaching through and across for a unity that will be all the richer because it embraces the difference.

At this early stage of the argument, it seems useful to make some distinctions. The first is between diversity and division. Diversity in religion is simply difference – difference in belief, in liturgy, in spirituality, in the application of moral principles, in vocation and so on. It will be a main thesis of this book that diversity is not only legitimate but something good, to be prized and maintained. Unfortunately, diversity has often passed into division. The differences have become hardened, communication has broken down and the spirit of pride, exclusiveness and bigotry takes over. Even division, one must concede, has sometimes been inevitable and even justifiable in the history of the church. Sometimes a point of view has been so far out that it constituted a threat to the integrity of the Christian faith as a whole, and could not be tolerated within the church. Sometimes a central ecclesiastical authority has been so overweening that a dissident group has had no alternative but to secede. But always, in such cases, both sides suffer and the church as a whole suffers.

2

While diversity is to be maintained, division is to be overcome.

One must likewise distinguish between different kinds of unity. There is the unity of origin, the given unity. This is nothing less than Jesus Christ himself, the head of the church. Something of this unity of origin persists among all who call themselves Christians. But there is also the unity of the end, the eschatological unity – though we should notice that ideally this is not just the unity of the church but the unity of all mankind in the kingdom of God. This eschatological unity is not the recovery of a unity that the church is supposed to have formerly enjoyed and has now lost. It is a far richer unity that will gather up all the diversities of traditions and individuals, all the riches that have been unpacked and developed from the original given in the ages of the church's pilgrimage.

It is worth recalling that from the very beginning the Christian church has been characterized by unity and diversity and even by division, and that the kind of situation described in the opening paragraphs of this chapter is a fairly typical one.

The unity is already attested by the use of such words as 'church' and 'Christianity'. These words have admittedly no precisely definable reference. They refer to vast complex phenomena spread out through space and time and having, as it were, rough edges. They are comparable to such words as 'Europe' and 'Buddhism'. Yet these words have some content. They draw our attention to historical configurations which can be distinguished because of some homogeneity, some common characteristics, although there are unclear borders. How, for instance, would one try to delimit the boundaries of the church? If we make baptism the criterion, then we would have to leave out the Quakers and the Salvation Army, though they are undoubtedly Christians. If we make right belief (orthodoxy) the criterion, then we could leave out some of the more heterodox sects, both ancient and modern. But these so-called 'heretics' belong, in a sense, to the church, in so far as they are by-products of Christianity and define themselves with reference to it. In any case, how does one fix the minimum of right belief that would entitle a particular group to inclusion? There is the serious danger that one may manipulate the formula to ensure such inclusions and exclusions as one has already decided on *a priori* grounds. At the time of its formation in 1948, the World Council of Churches attempted to draw the line by declaring that it 'is composed of churches which acknowledge Jesus Christ as God and Saviour'. Presumably this would exclude Unitarians. The formula seems simple enough, but it was not long before Rudolf Bultmann demonstrated its ambiguous and unsatisfactory nature.[1] It has since been expanded by a mention of the Trinity.

The rather vague unity implied in our talk of the 'church' constitutes a historical given, while the attempts to spell out the criteria qualifying for inclusion in the church may be considered attempts to translate the historical given into a theological given. But although there are doubtful borderline cases, if we consider the core, so to speak, comprising the vast majority of Christians, we find there an already existing unity which is quite substantial. Jesus Christ himself is the foundation of that unity. However scholars may disagree over the extent of our knowledge about him, no one doubts that the church came into being as a result of his teaching and career, and indeed it is the continuous existence of the church over nineteen centuries that is our chief evidence for the reality of Jesus himself. He made such an impression that there grew up a community confessing that 'Jesus Christ is Lord' (Phil. 2.11) and, however differently this primitive confession may be understood by different people today, it is still the essential bond that holds the church together. Then there is the New Testament. It provides us with the early church's testimony to Jesus Christ and with an account of how it understood itself as the community which he had called. It is truly remarkable that among the great mass of Christians for most of their history the same books have been received as canonical, and this is a very important unifying factor. Again, among the great majority, the distinctive sacraments of baptism and the eucharist are observed. One could go on and say something about the common ground in the matters of creeds and

4

ministry, but then we would be moving into more controversial areas, so for the moment we simply point to that solid core of given unity constituted by the acknowledgment of the Lordship of Christ, mediated through the word and sacraments.

Not only was there unity in the church from the beginning, there was also a *consciousness* of unity, and this consciousness was itself one of the constitutive factors in the church. We may believe that the primitive church is correctly portrayed in Acts as a community of sharing and that 'the company of those who believed were of one heart and soul' (Acts 4.32). It is in contrast to the divisions formerly prevailing among them that Paul tells the Christian disciples, 'You are all one in Christ Jesus' (Gal. 3.28) and this is only one of many references in his letters to the unity of Christians. Through baptism, they are united in one body through the one Spirit (I Cor. 12.8). The Fourth Gospel too stresses the unity of the disciples, though rather as a unity which in its fullness lies ahead than as a unity already realized. Jesus' reiterated prayer is 'that they may be one . . . that they may become perfectly one' (John 17.22–3). This consciousness of unity, attested in different parts of the New Testament, eventually becomes an essential element in the church's self-definition, as one of the four notes of the church listed in the Nicene creed: 'We believe one holy catholic and apostolic church.'

But it is quite clear that diversity too was present in the church from the beginning. We have spoken of Jesus Christ as the foundation of unity, but we cannot speak of Christ without already finding him interpreted in one way or another. We do not encounter him directly, but as mediated through the scriptures and the church. Already in the New Testament there are different presentations of Christ – the Pauline Christ, the synoptic Christ, the Johannine Christ. Each of the titles applied to Jesus – Messiah, Son of Man, Son of God, Lord, Word and so on – contains within itself the seeds of a definite type of christology. Certainly, these different interpretations do not contradict one another in any fundamental way, but they cannot easily be combined. To borrow an expression from Don Cupitt, there is 'one Jesus, many

5

Christs'. He writes: 'Jesus has been seen as moralist, prophet, apocalyptist, hero, redeemer, priest and king.'[2]

Not only is there a plurality of interpretations of Christ in the New Testament, there is, more generally, a plurality of theologies. Modern New Testament scholarship has made us acutely aware of this, and has shattered the supposition that there was an original clear and unified deposit of faith which subsequently was broken up. 'Early doctrine,' writes Maurice Wiles, 'was never a simple, coherent statement of faith which can be conceived as the compact seed from which all subsequent doctrine is an organic growth.'[3] On the practical side, there was a plurality of life styles, vocations and forms of spirituality among Christians. 'There are varieties of gifts, but the same Spirit; and there are varieties of service, but the same Lord; and there are varieties of working, but it is the same God who inspires them all in every one' (I Cor. 12.4). So Paul acknowledges the diversity, but sees it within a unity, and goes on to compare this diversity-in-unity with a living body.

The diversities, both theological and practical, resulted from the beginning in different kinds of churches. The church appears differently in the Pauline epistles, in Matthew's gospel and in Luke–Acts, to name only three areas of the New Testament. Admittedly, one must not exaggerate the differences. There is, shall we say, a family resemblance among the churches and it may even be possible, as Rudolf Schnackenburg has suggested, to discern certain essential characteristics that belong to all the New Testament churches, thereby 'attaining a deeper grasp of the one nature of the church'.[4] But for the moment I wish to emphasize the diversity. The traditional tendency was to play down the differences, to attempt to harmonize apparent discrepancies and, generally speaking, to idealize the early history of the church. Recent scholarship may have gone too far in the opposite direction in dwelling on the pluralism in the New Testament. But the time had come for redressing the balance and acknowledging frankly the differences in belief and practice that have characterized the church from the beginning. These differences are not to be regretted. They testify to the

6

richness and manysidedness of Christian faith and life, and they also provide possibilities for development.

This book will try to defend legitimate diversity, and will accord to diversity a higher value than has usually been set upon it. But it must be stressed that unity and diversity belong together in the church. Both are essential to its life and health. Where the tensions between unity and diversity are experienced, the church is likely to be alive and adventurous. A stark unity freezes the church and inhibits development. A sheer diversity would dissipate the church and cause her to disappear. Only unity and diversity together can be fruitful.

We should notice that division also appeared at a very early stage. Sometimes, it appears, the diversities could not be maintained within the unity and separation took place. The clearest instance in the New Testament is found in the First Epistle of John. This epistle lays great stress on love among the brethren, but it is quite uncompromising in its condemnation of a group of people of apparently gnostic tendencies. They had left the church, or been driven out of it, and their error was to teach that the Christ is not to be identified with the human Jesus (I John 2.22). This is certainly a difference going far beyond the differences between, let us say, the Pauline churches and the church at Jerusalem. But then one is faced with the very difficult question: At what point does a difference become so acute that it breaks the unity of the church and must lead to separation? It might be thought that the beliefs of the gnostic sectaries mentioned in I John were so subversive of the central Christian doctrine of the incarnation that division and separation were the only possible courses. There have to be some limits to diversity. Today, no doubt, our tendency is to be more permissive, but our situation is different from that of the late first century when the church was struggling to gain a foothold and dared not compromise its teaching. Yet even today we are not delivered from the difficult question about the limits of diversity, for if every opinion and every practice that claims to be Christian is permitted to shelter under the umbrella of the one church, then Christianity becomes so diffuse and ill-defined as to be deprived of any significance.

7

Throughout the church's history the two tendencies, the one towards unity, the other towards diversity, have been at work. Sometimes their tension has been fruitful, sometimes it has been destructive. Sometimes the one tendency has been stronger, sometimes the other. Sometimes the drive towards diversity has led to bitter divisions, sometimes the desire to realize unity has produced centralized authority, imposed uniformity and an infringement of legitimate freedoms.

The oscillation can be traced through most of the centuries of Christian history. In the early centuries the church was plagued by a seemingly never-ending series of heresies and schisms, though many of the heresies had their elements of truth. Then came the gradual separation of East and West, culminating in the breach of 1054. In the Middle Ages, the church of the West, in spite of its imposing centralized structure, was far from enjoying unity, for not only were there various fringe movements breaking away, there was the unedifying spectacle of schism at the very centre as pope quarrelled with antipope and anathemas and excommunications were freely exchanged. At the Reformation, new breaches occurred, and the national and regional churches of the West, Lutheran, Anglican and Reformed, embarked on an existence separate from Rome. Each of these churches tried to consolidate religious unity (or uniformity) within its own territory, and there were even moves to bring the churches of the Reformation together. But the rise of democracy and the principle of religious toleration led to new breaks and the multiplication of denominations.

But then the tide began to turn once more. As George H. Tavard has shown, for about two hundred years there have been significant and gradually mounting efforts towards a new manifestation of Christian unity, so that there was, as he puts it, an 'incubation period' before the emergence of the contemporary ecumenical movement.[5] But it has been in the twentieth century that the ecumenical movement has gained its full momentum. To begin with, the stirrings were among the Protestant churches, and were motivated especially by the problems that divisions were causing in Christian missions overseas. Then, with Vatican II, the Roman Catholic Church committed itself to the ecumenical movement. Events have moved fast, and today the many churches, communions, denominations of Christians are enjoying an era of friendship and co-operation that is probably unprecedented. All this has brought a new strength and a new hope to the church, and there can be no turning back to the days of hostility and isolationism.

But what is the way forward? Everyone acknowledges that there is still a long way to go towards Christian unity. The danger, however, is that in the present preoccupation with unity – one might almost say, the prevailing ecumenical euphoria – one may lose sight of that diversity which is equally important for the church's well-being. The only worthwhile unity will be one which gathers up all the enriching diversity of the varying Christian traditions, and how this can be done needs much thought, patience and charity. There can be no easy road that will lead us to the realization in any depth of the goal: *All One in Christ Jesus*.

2

Christianity and Pluralism

We are nowadays all familiar with the word 'pluralism'. It is a prestigious word. Pluralism is taken to be the mark of a modern society as distinct from a primitive one. It could even be said that the index of a society's maturity is its pluralism, its capacity not only to tolerate but to maintain and even to encourage the coexistence within its bosom of diverse groups of people. According to Jacques Maritain, 'the first central and concrete fact which imposes itself as characteristic of a modern civilization as opposed to medieval civilization is that the self-same civilization admits into its bosom religious diversity'.[1]

We have moved far from the days when everyone in a country was required to adhere to precisely the same religious beliefs and forms of worship. Nowadays, in any free society, it is recognized that there will be diversity. This diversity includes not only differences of religion but, in developed countries, various non-religious ideologies. The old homogeneous societies have been broken up and diversified, and this process is likely to continue at an increased rate in the future, because people nowadays have so much more mobility. Last century Europeans moved to other continents and settled there, and they still do; but this century Indians migrate to England, Turks to Germany, Algerians to France. The peoples of the world are being mixed up in many ways and are no longer distributed in homogeneous, geographically delimited blocs as in earlier times.

Maritain mentioned diversity in religion as the chief difference between a modern pluralist society and a medieval society, and it is true that both in the Middle Ages and in the time after the Reformation religion was, from a sociological point of view, used as a cement for holding society together. But its position today is more likely to be marginal. The pluralism of a contemporary society is cultural, political and sometimes racial as well as religious. For instance, in the United States, which may be regarded as the most advanced pluralist society in the world today, it is the racial issue that is proving most difficult. The relation began through the subjection and oppression of the African section of the population. Then there was a movement towards integration. The blacks were to be brought into the mainstream of American life, they were to be given the same opportunities as whites and to participate in the prevailing American way of life. But soon the younger members of the black community were discovering that this meant a loss of identity. They were being asked to accept a pattern of American life that had already been decided exclusively by the white majority. So the pendulum began to swing the other way towards a new kind of separatism in which the black community seeks to develop its own distinctive values and life styles, believing that only so can freedom and dignity be gained for those who were so long deprived of them. No doubt many further adjustments and even conflicts will take place before the United States can reach the goal of a society which, though one, will maximize the freedom and distinctiveness of the myriad groups and individuals who constitute it – before, in effect, the right way is found to realize the dream of the founding fathers, *e pluribus unum*.

These remarks on pluralism make it clear that its problems are very much like those of ecumenism, though on a larger scale and in a more complex form. How do we combine unity and diversity, law and liberty? Only among the emerging and therefore still insecure nations of the world do we still find the attempt to impose a rigid unity. The more sophisticated peoples have long since turned their backs on that, but they have now become worried that the drive to maximize difference and permissiveness may lead to a final disintegration. It is within the context of this general search for a pluralist society that the problem of ecumenism is to be understood. In one sense, the two quests are parallel, yet the relation is more complicated than that, for the religious, cultural, political and racial issues all cut across and influence one another.

At first sight, it might seem that ecumenism, as the quest for unity, is moving in opposition to the pluralistic drive towards freedom, differentiation and permissiveness. Certainly, there could be no thought of trying to set up once more the monolithic religious unities of the past, whether the unity of the medieval church or the national and regional unities that were established after the Reformation on the principle, *cuius regio, eius religio*. Any kind of unity envisaged must be different from the unities of the past (often imposed and merely superficial) and must take full account of the freedoms that have been so painfully won in the struggles that have brought us from homogeneous to pluralist societies.

To be sure, advocates of church union schemes often assure us that they are not aiming at uniformity. But I do not think that they have really taken seriously the extent of pluralism today or its legitimacy. This point can be illustrated from the attempts to set up united national or regional churches. This is an idea that smacks too much of the old *cuius regio, eius religio* formula. For instance, it has been proposed that in Great Britain there will be three autonomous churches, English, Scottish and Welsh, each uniting in itself the denominations at present existing in each of the three countries. It is anticipated that these three united churches would differ quite widely in theology, polity and liturgy, reflecting the historical and cultural differences of the three countries, though it is hoped that there would also be full mutual recognition among them. What is not envisaged is that there could be two or more autonomous churches in the same geographical area. But the attempt to limit differences to those that can be defined in national or regional terms is not adequate to the freedom that may be rightly expected in a pluralistic age. The concept of united national and regional churches goes back to the days of homogeneous societies geographically demarcated and, even so, represents a tradition that has proved itself hostile to freedom and openness.

To permit a plurality of different autonomous Christian

communities only on geographical grounds is needlessly restrictive of legitimate freedom and counter to the principles of a mature pluralistic society. There are nowadays just as compelling grounds for having two or more autonomous churches *within* Scotland or *within* England as there are for having one north of the border and another south of it; and it is possible to visualize these churches as complementary to each other and as united by the same ties of mutual recognition and close co-operation that might subsist between two national churches.

At this point, however, it may be desirable to examine more closely the concept of pluralism. Is pluralism merely something that has developed with the rise of democratic societies, so that it may not be applicable to the Christian church which, so Christians believe, is more than a human society? Or does pluralism have deeper roots and possibly a theological justification? We have in fact seen in the first chapter that diversity as well as unity has characterized the church from the beginning.

It is worth noting that the use of the word 'pluralism' to describe a certain type of society – the way we have been using the word in this chapter up till now – is very recent. In an older usage, the word had philosophical, not socio-logical, import. It was in a philosophical context that I first met the word 'pluralism' myself. 'Pluralism' was the opposite of 'monism'. Pluralism was advocated by philosophers of emprical temperament, such as William James, whose book, *A Pluralistic Universe*, was based on a series of lectures given in Oxford, at that time a stronghold of monistic idealism.

Monism is the doctrine that in spite of the appearance of multiplicity and change, there is only one reality. Monism is therefore a belief that the real is static, finished, perfected. The early Greek philosopher Parmenides is generally held to have been a monist, teaching that reality is a unity excluding all change and diversity: 'What is, is, and it is impossible for it not to be.' Another example is the Indian philosopher Sankara, who taught that the sole reality is the eternal *brahma*, while finite beings and events constitute *maya*, a kind of illusory surface play. Similarly, the absolute idealism popular in England at the beginning of the century held that ultimate reality belongs only to the timeless unchanging absolute, and that sensory spatio-temporal experience is by contrast appearance.

Pluralism, on the other hand, is not to be understood as the doctrine that there is just a sheer multiplicity of facts, a swarm of unrelated particulars. Such a multiverse, if one may so speak, would be unintelligible and absurd. But pluralism is the belief that the world is dynamic, unfinished, open. Therefore the pluralist takes individuals and particulars seriously, and he takes time and becoming seriously. Let William James be the spokesman: 'The pluralistic world is more like a federal republic than like an empire or a kingdom. However much may be collected, however much may report itself as present at any effective centre of consciousness or action, something else is self-governed and absent and unreduced to unity.'[2] This means, of course, that the pluralist view of the world will never have the tidiness of the monistic view. But is this not much more like the world we know, both the world around us and our own human existence, a world in which there are always loose ends and everything is always on its way?

The Christian understanding of the world is neither monism nor an extreme pluralism (if that means a doctrine of sheer multiplicity) but it accords very well with a moderate pluralism. The Christian doctrine of creation teaches that all things have a single scource, God, and that therefore all things tend to a single end, which is also God. But the created beings are real, and not just appearance. God himself has created these beings, and has given them their own reality and even a degree of independence and freedom. He was not content (so we may speak) to dwell within himself but shared the gift of being with his creatures. It would seem that in his creation, God has aimed at the utmost diversity. Even in our little corner of the universe, the richness and variety of the creatures fills us with wonder. Perhaps most amazing of all is the seemingly infinite variety of human beings. Billions of them have lived on earth, yet each one is a unique person. Each one, again, has his own needs and his own way of responding to God, and we

14

may believe that God on his part reaches out to his creatures in many ways, taking account of their differing modes of response. Incidentally, it was again William James who opened up the fascinating vista of different religious responses in his classic work, *The Varieties of Religious Experience*. Near the beginning of that book, he utters the warning: 'The theorizing mind tends always to the oversimplification of its materials. This is the root of all that absolutism and one-sided dogmatism by which both philosophy and religion have been infested.'[3]

The fact then that God himself seems to maximize variety in his creation and, more especially, the fact that he meets men and women in many modes of experience suited to their differing needs provides a theological justification for pluralism in the Christian community. Yet we have to remember that the doctrine of creation is compatible with a moderate, not an unlimited, pluralism, and in the church too, even if it is right to encourage difference, there cannot be disruptive or wanton individualism.

After the breakdown of the unitary churches, whether pre-Reformation or post-Reformation, denominationalism emerged as the expression of the new pluralism, and it still holds the field. It has become fashionable nowadays to denounce denominationalism as a very bad arrangement, and I would agree that the time has come for us to press on towards some new form of church life that will better express in visible form the unity of the church. But this should not blind us to the fact that for several centuries denominationalism did cope reasonably well with the demands for religious freedom and Christian diversity. As Gordon Kaufman has written, 'although denominational differences in perspective and mode of life have often led to regrettable consequences, they should not be regarded as wholly unfortunate. For the denominations are living witnesses to the importance of the insight into Christian faith which each knows. Within the limits of human finitude such divisions, with the resultant conversations and struggles, may well be the essential socio-logical expression of the necessity to correct the onesidedness of every interpretation and every tradition so that the fullness of the whole Christian faith is not lost.'[4] Certainly the wealth of traditions that the denominations have preserved must not be lost, even if the old structures have to change.

It is interesting to notice too that Christianity seems to have thrived much more vigorously in countries where there has been denominational diversity than in countries where the great majority of the people are embraced within a single church. This fact makes very questionable the statement sometimes made that people are kept away from the church because of its divisions. Let me give some examples. There are still a few countries where the old unitary churches have survived almost intact. In Spain, for instance, 97% of the people belong to the Roman Catholic Church which was hardly affected by the Reformation. But could anyone say that this has been a healthy state of affairs? For, at least until very recently, the Spanish church, enjoying its near monopoly, has been highly intolerant and reactionary. In Sweden, on the other hand, we have an example of a post-Reformation establishment. The Church of Sweden claims 98% of the people, and perhaps it is a sufficient commentary on this to mention that an opinion poll shows only 60% of Swedes professing belief in God. The Church of Sweden has maintained a remarkable tradition of fine scholarship, but its influence on the ordinary life of the people is minimal, and one suspects that this is not unconnected with its position as the only considerable Christian body in the country. By way of contrast, the United States has a very large number of denominations, none of which has a dominant position in the country. 'Worship next Sunday in the church of your choice!' is an exhortation that can be seen displayed on posters and on the page of the newspaper carrying the church advertisements. There is a kind of raw individualism in this, yet when one considers what a vastly diversified country America is, then it is important that God's word should be addressed to all these different groups and individuals in a great many ways. Certainly, the American churches are far more vigorous and lively than are the churches in most of the technologically advanced nations. Let us agree that American religion can be criticized on many grounds. Nevertheless, when all has been said, there is much that is adventurous, imaginative, reconciling and valuable in the life of the churches of the United States, and it is hard to believe that this vigour does not in part arise from the diversity of the country's Christianity and the constant interactions among the different groups.

However, as I have already indicated, I do not wish to defend denominationalism as a permanent feature of the church's life. I believe it fulfilled a useful function in its day, but now we must be prepared to look beyond it. The trouble about denominationalism is that it went beyond diversity to division, and division still remains to some extent, even if most of the old bitterness and rivalry has now been overcome. Yet if we are to move beyond denominationalism, this move must be in such a manner that the diversities of the several traditions are maintained. The many options in theology and spirituality that have been available in the past must continue to be available in the future, and perhaps we shall need more rather than less. As Stephen Sykes has remarked: 'If God's work is to be done in a world of vastly differing patterns of personal and social life, we must expect men to be called to live in different traditions of piety and devotion. To attempt to conform all Christians to a uniform ideal would be a gross mistake and danger.'[5] It must be remembered too that the different Christian traditions – Orthodox, Lutheran, Methodist, Anglican and so on – has each a certain integrity and, like an art style, cannot be mixed with other traditions without loss of its distinctive appeals.

Can all these options be maintained within one church, rather than scattered through the denominations? Obviously, a multiform church would need to be very different from the unitary churches of the past. But we strike against further problems. The real evil of division is not diversity but the bitterness and lovelessness to which it can lead, and this can happen within a single church structure as well as between denominations. At the present time, for instance, while the bitterness of denominational differences has receded to almost negligible proportions, new divisions have arisen that spread through all the denominations. The Roman Catholic Church is experiencing an acute tension between progressive and conservative elements, and the same kind of polarization is to be found in other Christian churches. Clearly, the churches need both radicals and conservatives, and also a lot of people in between who will help to reconcile the extremes. But the point is that a single ecclesiastical structure will not ensure the overcoming of division and lovelessness, and it has not done so in the past. The historian Latourette has written: 'The inclusive structure of the Catholic Church has not ensured the bond of love which is central to Christian unity as conceived in the New Testament.'[6] In stronger terms, Ian Henderson has declared: 'The projected solution of the contradiction of Christian lovelessness by means of a series of ecclesiastical mergers is so grotesquely superficial that in the end it can only exacerbate the problem, and has indeed already begun to do so.'[7]

What then is to be the solution? We must look for a way of unifying the denominations that will be sufficiently open in its texture to respect the integrity and autonomy of each of the participating traditions. Or, to put the matter differently, we must be as much in earnest with pluralism as we are with unity, recognizing that both have their justification in Christian theology.

The trouble is that as soon as one begins to consider structures, one cannot avoid the question of power. And as soon as the question of power arises, then one has also to face the temptations of power. The church itself is composed of sinful persons who are by no means immune to the temptations of power – indeed, from what I have been able to observe, I would say that ecclesiastical politics are quite as ruthless as anything that goes on in Parliament or Congress. It was a well-founded distrust of power that led Ian Henderson to make his criticisms of the ecumenical movement in his controversial book, *Power without Glory*. He said himself that he had presented his criticisms in exaggerated form, but his aim was to alert the church to real dangers.

One of the most worrying features of the churches and of the ecumenical movement in particular has been the tremendous growth in recent years of an ecclesiastical bureaucracy which, one fears, maintains only a very tenuous contact with the actual life of the church in the parishes. There has come into being a kind of ecclesiastical jet set, whose members seem always to be on the point of departing for conferences in Jakarta or Uppsala, or just getting back from other conferences in Accra or Caracas. I am reminded of what Solzhenitsyn says about a member of the Russian general staff in his indictment of bureaucracy in *August 1914*: 'The secret of his success had been movement – departure, travel, arrival, then off again – not fighting.'[8]

Surely sociologist Bryan Wilson greatly exaggerates when he writes: 'The forces of ecumenism are clerical forces . . . we witness the struggles of a professional for survival in the Protestant countries of Europe.'[9] I do not myself think that the professional ecclesiastic is consciously a power seeker. But inevitably he does come to think of things in terms of efficiency, control, resources, economy and so on, with the result that considerations of theology and spirituality are pushed into the background. He even begins to use the language of big business and to talk about denominational 'mergers'. The rise of this bureaucracy is accompanied by a pressure towards conformity and a corresponding threat to diversity and freedom. When this begins to happen, it may well be the duty of the Christian to defend the legitimate interests of pluralism against the drive towards uniformity.

At any rate, the protection of diversity would seem to require something a good deal more complex than the absorption of the denominations into a unitary church, which would be, in fact, itself a new denomination. As Paul Tillich has observed, 'neither the ecumenical nor any future movement can conquer the ambiguity of unity and division in the churches' historical existence. Even if it were able to produce the United Churches of the World, and even if all latent churches were converted to this unity, new divisions would appear. The dynamics of life, the tendency to preserve the holy even when it has become obsolete, the ambiguities implied in the sociological existence of the churches and, above all, the prophetic criticism and demand for reformation would bring about new and, in many cases, spiritually justified divisions.'[10]

3

Practical Ecumenism

In the two opening chapters of this book I have sketched out something of the dialectic of Christian unity and Christian diversity, and since the thrust is currently towards unity, I have stressed the claims of diversity and insisted that heed must be given to these claims, otherwise we shall end up with a false unity, like some of the unities of the past, or else we shall find ourselves being driven into new divisions. The goal is clear enough. It is a form of unity in which there will be (to quote the words of Pope Paul VI in his inaugural address at the second session of Vatican II) 'a large variety of languages, of ritual forms, of historical traditions, of local prerogatives, of spiritual currents, of legitimate institutions and preferred activities'. If we ponder these words of the Pope, we shall soon recognize that they allow for a great deal of diversity indeed.

But while the goal has been set, the way towards it has still to be worked out. The remainder of this book will be mostly concerned with considering ways towards the goal and the overcoming of obstacles standing in the way. In this chapter I shall begin with what lies nearest at hand – practical ecumenism. In certain respects, this is to begin with what is easiest, for there are things that can be done and should be done right away, since they do not depend on the solution of any intricate theological problems. Yet it would be equally true to say that we are beginning with what is most difficult, for the problem of the church at any time is the gap between its theological profession and the practical working out of its faith. Especially at the present time, when the task of commending Christian belief to the modern mind is such a difficult one, it is Christian faith in practice that is still able to make an impact. Of course, practice and belief are closely intertwined, and cannot finally be separated.

It seems to be an almost universally accepted principle of spirituality that the growth and deepening of the Christian life come about when men and women are not consciously striving to achieve such growth and deepening but are looking out beyond themselves. The spiritual director tries to get his charges to look out beyond the horizons of their own lives, and as they do so they are, so to speak, stretched and they increase in stature. On the other hand, if they keep looking inward, trying to measure their progress and anxiously wondering whether they are making any progress at all or may even be slipping back, then growth seems to be arrested. This is the familiar paradox of the spiritual life. It is the man who can lose himself and forget himself who gains in stature; while the spiritual valetudinarian, striving over earnestly to be good or saintly or whatever, remains wrapped up in himself and may even turn spirituality into a form of egotism.

Empirical psychology teaches in more general terms a law of reversed effort, that is to say, there are situations where, the harder we try and the more attention we pay to what we are doing, the less likely we are to succeed. R. H. Thouless visualizes a situation in which one is asked to walk along a plank that has been elevated to an uncomfortable level above the ground. He says: 'You will find, under these conditions, that the harder you try to prevent yourself from falling off, the more certainly you will do so. Your only chance of performing the task successfully is to adopt a method which reduces to a minimum both your fear of a fall and your voluntary effort to keep on the plank; in other words, you must think neither about the height nor about the effort necessary to keep on the plank, but only about getting to the other end.'[1] There we have the important point – getting to the other end. Preoccupation with ourselves is no help, but rather the reverse.

What is true of the individual is even more true with respect to a social entity. Reinhold Niebuhr once wrote that 'the community is the frustration as well as the realization of individual life'.[2] For while it is only in a community and along with others that the individual can bring his ideals to realization, he is constantly frustrated by the fact (which Niebuhr never tired of stressing) that the group is always more self-centred and less sensitive to moral demands that the individual. This is true in the Christian life. We meet individual Christians who are capable of going to great lengths of love, self-forgetfulness and self-sacrifice. They walk along the plank, so to speak, with their eyes fixed on the goal, giving little direct thought to how they are performing at any given time. The self-conscious saint would be a contradiction in terms. But we never find this self-forgetfulness in the corporate group which constitutes a church. The churches are almost notoriously introspective. They spend endless time discussing their own inner workings, and then express surprise that they seem to be making so little impact on the world around. No doubt it is impossible for the corporate group to achieve what some individuals can achieve in this regard, but one might hope that it could do better than it does.

It would be a fair criticism of the ecumenical movement – and one which many ecumenists would be willing to accept – that it has been too inward-looking and too self-involved. Churchmen have talked to churchmen about the churches. Sociologists know well that when groups of this kind are set up and meet regularly, they develop an atmosphere of understanding, they evolve something like a private language and indeed they begin to build up a little world of their own, determined by the interests and values that have brought them together. Those who engage in such talks are often surprised and even somewhat hurt when they find that the results are received with coolness in the church at large. This is often attributed to the fact that there is no grass-roots participation, but there is more to it than that. It arises primarily from the introspective nature of such talks. And if such talks fail to find much response in the churches themselves, they make even less impact on the wider world.

Let me not be misunderstood. I am not saying that the churches should not talk with one another about the nature of the church itself. There is a place for this, and some of the talks that have gone on under ecumenical auspices have been very helpful and illuminating – though I think the best of them have been the relatively open, theologically oriented talks between the representatives of worldwide communions, rather than the somewhat restricted exchanges between national or regional groups of churches aimed at negotiating the basis for a united church in their area. But what is important is that inter-church activity should be set in a wider context. We have over the years invested a colossal amount of time and resources into these inter-church exercises when perhaps the priority should have been elsewhere. The focus of ecumenism needs to be changed or, at least, the amount of importance which we assign to its several focuses needs to be shifted. It has always been a temptation to the churches to look inward and to become preoccupied with their own life. It is ironical that they should still be doing this even although we nowadays hear a great deal about mission and it is even argued that unity is needed for the sake of mission. The time has come for the churches to look out together on the world. It might be surprising how much unity would develop unconsciously through a common response to the challenges of contemporary society. The unity which is so elusive when churchmen talk to each other may begin to burgeon when they are able to engage in common practical concerns. Furthermore, this would be a unity with true existential foundations, rather than one that has come about as the blueprint devised by a high-powered ecclesiastical commission. If this practical, scarcely conscious growing into unity were to take place over a period of time at all levels in the churches, then a foundation would have been laid that would also ensure that grass-roots preparation and interest which so often seems to be lacking in ecumenical affairs. The more theoretical aspects of ecumenism are going to be exciting and credible only after the churches have shown that they do have a will to work together on the practical tasks of bringing more abundant life to the world.

What I have called in this chapter 'practical ecumenism' has also been known in recent years by the expression 'secular ecumenism'. The name does not matter very much. Yet this adjective 'secular' does draw attention to some features of the kind of ecumenical effort we have in mind, and to reflect

23

on it for a moment will help to fill in some details in the picture. There are at least three points that seem to call for mention.

First, secular ecumenism is distinguished by the adjective from official, church sponsored ecumenism. This secular ecumenism is not always informal. It may be on a large scale and highly organized. I suppose Christian Aid would be an example. But the more typical forms of secular ecumenism are quite informal and local. Some of the most meaningful ecumenism occurs when people of very diverse Christian backgrounds, Catholic, Protestant and other, get together and perhaps also bring into their number Jews, humanists and people with no very clear religious opinions at all. What joins them together is a desire to do what they can to meet some particular need of which they have become aware and about which they are concerned. That need may be to provide better schools or housing in their area and to bring pressure to bear on the appropriate authority; or it may be to provide services for old or sick people; or it may be to reconcile hostile groups in the community; or it may be to provide recreational or cultural facilities for young people; or it may be any of a hundred other things. (Usually, it will be to fill some gap that is not taken care of by the public authority, and if in due course the public authority can be persuaded to sponsor that particular service, then the *ad hoc* voluntary group will probably break up and its members will turn to other matters.) In this secular kind of ecumenism, those who have come together are probably not even contemplating any theological *rapprochement*. In the context of their service, they will probably have very little awareness of denomination, and perhaps the Christian members of the group will have little awareness of being distinct from the non-Christians. To be sure, they may be motivated by the reconciling message of Christianity and the vision of God's kingdom coming on earth. But the basis for this ecumenism is not a nicely worked out ecclesiology or even a doctrine of redemption but simply that natural morality which is common to all men by virtue of their humanity. The Christian members of the group do not even forcibly baptize the others by

24

calling them 'anonymous Christians' or anything of the sort. It is enough that they are human beings. As Paul tells us, there are many people who have neither the law of Christ nor the law of Moses but whose actions make it clear that they have 'a law written in their hearts' (Rom. 2.15). As Christians believe, they all participate in the fundamental moral law that is founded in God and imparted to his human creatures with his image. From a Christian point of view, this non-exclusive secular ecumenism is not just good works apart from the gospel but a common obedience. Its basis is not a non-Christian humanism but the recognition that all humanity is the creation of God and the concern of God, and has a share in that image of God that is perfectly expressed in Christ.

The second point is that in secular ecumenism, the effort of those involved is directed outward on the world rather than on the church or churches. The primary aim of the secular ecumenist is the unity of mankind. This type of ecumenism therefore comes as a timely reminder that the end of history, according to Christian belief, is not the church but the kingdom of heaven, and this is a more inclusive concept, gathering up both church and world in an eschatological unity. Our primary aim should not be the unity of the church. We look beyond that to the unity of mankind. But in pursuing that greater unity, it may well be that the unity of the church will come more quickly as a by-product or as a provisional stage on the way than it would have done if we had concentrated directly on ecclesiastical unity. The really dangerous and explosive divisions among men today are not (except in a very few areas) religious differences. The deep, bitter divisions that threaten the whole future of mankind run today along the lines that separate race from race, nation from nation, class from class. It is along these lines, above all, that the reconciling work of the church is desperately needed. By comparison, Christian divisions seem polite and gentlemanly – whatever they may have been in the past. Romans and Lutherans, Anglicans and Methodists, are not usually out to murder each other! The most urgent work of reconciliation lies elsewhere. Sometimes, however, church ecumenists seem to lose sight of this. The type of ecumenism that aims to bring into being national united churches in each country seems to me quite misguided. The last thing the world needs is a series of national churches reduplicating the political divisions that already exist, and in some cases breaking up the international Christian communions (Roman, Anglican, Lutheran, etc.) which transcend national and racial borders. 'The Church,' wrote Cardinal Bea, 'feels itself intimately linked with all mankind and co-operates in the achieving of unity for mankind.'[3] This is something we must not be allowed to forget, and secular ecumenism forcibly reminds us of it by giving priority to the unity of mankind over ecclesiastical unity.

A third point to be learned from the secular ecumenists concerns the historical dimension that is inevitably met in the ecumenical quest. In the fullest sense, unity is an eschatological idea. But our own quest for unity takes place in the *saeculum*, in the unfolding of history. The full goal lies beyond history, but the way to it lies through history and there is no shortcut. It is through the freedom and creativity of history that man, the historical being, builds his communities and establishes his identities. Ray L. Hart makes the interesting point that attempts to construct a universal language, such as Esperanto, have failed because man cannot have a common language until he has a common history.[4] We must not make the mistake of putting together a synthetic Christianity which would similarly lack a historical rootage. Christians have been a long time growing into division, and we must expect that it will take them time to grow into unity. And that growth will be a costly one of practical service together, leading to a unity deeper than can come from discussions alone. D. M. Mac-Kinnon expressed the point by saying: 'We must not suggest that out of contrivance on the part of skilful and ingenious men what may only be won through a discipline of acceptance can by less costly methods be achieved almost in a few hours.'[5]

I have thought it right in this chapter to lay great stress on practical ecumenism as the first and foundational step towards the goal of unity-in-diversity and diversity-in-unity. This does not mean that I think we can sit lightly to the

26

theological questions, and these will bulk largely in most of the chapters that follow. Indeed, radical Christians who are impatient of theological niceties and lay all the stress on practical or secular ecumenism, may think that I am now going to bring in too much theology. I do not think this is the case, but I do agree that without a practical and costly basis in united striving for the unity and well-being of all mankind, a merely theoretical or institutional ecumenism lacks credibility. Much more has to be done by all the churches in this matter of practical ecumenism.

4

Ecumenical Theology

For a long time theology has been an ecumenical activity, and this is more the case today than ever before. Students of theology eagerly read the works of writers from many traditions and many countries and in some cases it might be hard to tell to what tradition a particular writer belongs from his handling of the major theological doctrines. In systematic theology, Rahner, Tillich, Bouyer, Barth, Pannenberg are studied everywhere. Likewise in biblical studies the work of Bultmann, Knox, Dodd, von Rad and others cuts across all denominational and national lines. Theological studies now go on in a worldwide community of scholars drawn from all the major churches. There is therefore today a sense in which all theology can be called ecumenical theology.

The expression 'ecumenical theology' will, however, often be understood in more restricted ways. Most commonly, perhaps, ecumenical theology is understood as the exploration of those theological issues which have been divisive in the past, with a view to finding whether a fresh approach can lead to a new reconciling understanding of the question. Such theology may be done by individuals or by groups and interconfessional bodies. I believe that such theology needs to be done, and more will be said about it. But obviously the dangers of an introspective attitude on the part of the churches, discussed in the last chapter, emerge again at this point, and there is today a considerable disillusionment with what may be called conventional ecumenical theology. Karl Rahner, for instance, asks: 'What has ecumenical theology really achieved up to now?' He replies: 'I confess to being for my part somewhat sceptical that anything very much has been achieved. This is not a purely subjective feeling – I am speaking from many years' experience of ecumenical dialogue with theological specialists in the various separated churches. There seems to me to be two quite different hazards in this whole under-taking. On the one hand, ecumenical dialogues among ordinary Christians tend to lose their way in a confessional relativism. Doctrines traditionally dividing the churches are passed over in an all too superficial and hasty way. The theological specialists, on the other hand, develop their ecumenical dialogue mostly within the area of the classical controversial doctrines, but hardly advance at all within the problematic.' Rahner goes on to argue that 'the most ecumeni-cal theology is that theology for the future which has to be worked out by all the churches, each from its own historically determined starting-point'.[1] What he means by a 'theology of the future' is quite simply a theology that will state the great themes of Christian faith in ways that come to grips with the strange new age which we are entering – the age of technology, cybernetics, the global unity of mankind and so on. Rahner obviously has an important point here, and it parallels in the theological sphere the argument we put for-ward in the last chapter in the practical sphere. In both cases, Christians are being asked to attend not to each other but to the problems that confront them all, in the hope that as they tackle these problems together, they will grow more and more into a unity which will be both existential and in-tellectual.

We should notice, however, that Rahner does not envisage the emergence of a theological consensus; or, at least, not a simple consensus. On the contrary, he seems to expect that we shall move increasingly into theological pluralism. He talks of the possibility of 'a number of theologies juxtaposed in a pluralist way, not contradicting each other, but not susceptible of being positively incorporated into a higher synthesis.'[2] I think myself this is a correct view of the matter. The progress of theology does not consist in moving towards a statement of doctrine that would be final and could be accepted by all as an adequate statement of truth. The dialectical character of theology precludes any such possibility, to say nothing of the historical and social conditioning of any statement. The progress of theology will take place rather through dialogue and through the confrontation and engagement of different and sometimes opposing views. It is through such dialogue that ecumenical theology can keep theology alive and forward-looking, whereas every 'consensus' is a temptation to call a halt to the theological quest for deeper understanding and to give the impression that one has 'arrived'.

A good illustration of what I have in mind would be the current thinking on the doctrine of God. Rahner does in fact acknowledge as a central problem of the 'theology of the future' the question of 'how theology can speak of God, and his existence in the midst of mankind, in such a way that the words can be understood by the men of today and tomorrow'.[3] When we consider how present-day theologians are thinking of God, we notice on the one hand a remarkable consensus. This may be due in part to a larger historical dialectic, in which the swing is currently against notions of God which emphasize his transcendence, otherness, majesty and, above all, his impassibility. So we find some theologians of existentialist tendency seeking to elucidate the doctrine of God by using Heidegger's philosophy of being (or some similar philosophy) with the result that God is brought very close to the world and its history. The process theologians turn to realist philosophers such as Whitehead and Hartshorne and develop a panentheism according to which God really is involved in temporal process and the struggle and suffering that go with it. Teilhard de Chardin's evolutionary world-view is another type of theism, powerfully influential in some Roman Catholic circles, and taking such an intensely sacramental view of the material universe that sometimes one seems very close to pantheism. Perhaps most remarkable of all is the shift taking place in the biblically based Protestant theology which continues the tradition of the Reformation, for whereas a mere generation ago the leaders of this type of thought (Barth, Brunner and others) were stressing the otherness and transcendence of God, some of its contemporary representatives (Jüngel and Moltmann are examples) seem to have brought God much closer to the struggles of history, and

Moltmann has even introduced the term panentheism into his theology of a God who suffers.[4] All this, I say, is a remarkable convergence. Yet, on the other hand, the differences among these various theological stances are very considerable and certainly preclude any synthesis. Some of these differences relate to the traditions of different churches and denominations, for instance, Catholic, Anglican and liberal Protestant theologians are prepared to give a role to natural theology and philosophical speculation, whereas the Reformation theologians set their faces firmly against metaphysical theism and claim to base their thinking about God on the revelation in Jesus Christ. But cutting across these differences arising from different ecclesiastical traditions are the differences arising from different philosophical influences, for instance, the contrast between the existentialist theologian's concern with man and the process theologian's concern with nature.

The situation I have described in this brief characterization of current thinking about God will not result in some vague 'consensus' – and if it did, theologians would have a duty to criticize it and to get theological thought going again. But we do have in those converging yet differentiated theologies rich material for deepening our understanding of God. It is this kind of situation which, I would believe in agreement with Rahner, constitutes the most important and promising kind of ecumenical theology. And it should be noted that I have mentioned only a few of the tributaries; one could have added Eastern Orthodox theology, the black theology of the United States, the emerging Indian Christian theology, the liberation theology of South America, and so on. Furthermore, what is said here about the doctrine of God could be paralleled with similar illustrations from the work being done on other major Christian doctrines. In the field of christology, for instance, there is a new concern to give adequate weight to the humanity of Christ without falling into the errors of adoptionism, and one can see this concern across the whole spectrum, in such writers as Rahner (Roman Catholic), Pannenberg (Lutheran), Meyendorff (Russian Orthodox), J. A. T. Robinson (Anglican). Yet although there is this convergence of approach and although this constitutes a difference from the

31

classical approach and can be considered characteristic of contemporary christologies, yet these contemporary christologies differ very much among themselves as each writer brings to bear on the problems the resources of his own tradition and again one is conscious that there could not be a synthesis. The fruitfulness of all this work lies both in the agreement and the differences.

While agreeing with Rahner that the most important ecumenical theology is this reflection upon and rethinking of the central Christian doctrines from a variety of viewpoints, I disagree when he suggests (as he seems to do) that there is no need to have alongside this fundamental theology a more explicitly ecumenical theology engaged in discussing and, if possible, reconciling some of the traditional matters of dispute that have led to divisions among Christians. It is, however, very important that we should have our priorities right, and this second kind of ecumenical theology should never become a major preoccupation and should always be clearly seen in the context of the wider theological endeavour.

The specifically ecumenical theology, that is to say, the type which aims primarily at reconciling doctrinal differences among the traditions, is, for the most part, concerned with those particular areas of theology where inter-church and inter-denominational differences have been most acute. Such areas are the doctrines of church, ministry and sacraments. Since there has always been broad agreement on the central doctrines of God, Christ, sin, salvation and so on, these have not usually come into the purview of a specifically ecumenical theology but have been assumed as a common background. But this is not always the case, for sometimes there have been serious divisions arising out of very central questions. For instance, Protestant theology has always maintained its own definite interpretation of the doctrine of justification, and this has been very much at the centre – Luther regarded it as the doctrine by which the church stands or falls. One of the most brilliant works in recent ecumenical theology is Hans Küng's *Justification*, in which he deals with Catholic and Protestant interpretations of the doctrine and, although there are different opinions about the success of his thesis, one must at least say that he has shown that the difference between the two traditions is blurred at a number of points and that the doctrine of justification does not seem to constitute an impassable barrier. Another fairly central matter on which there was for long supposed to be a radical difference between Catholics and Protestants is the nature of tradition and its role in Christian theology. Here the 'Dogmatic Constitution on Divine Revelation' of Vatican II and Yves Congar's *Tradition and Traditions* have been major influences in bridging the gap between the two sides. But in the main, the specifically ecumenical theology is concerned with ecclesiology and related matters.

This is a task which we cannot evade, even though we have agreed with Rahner that the most important ecumenical theology is of a different kind. But before we consider the task of a specifically ecumenical theology further, we must make ourselves fully aware of the dangers that attend it. We have seen already what some of these are. There is the danger of the churches becoming too introspective as they concentrate attention on ecclesiastical questions, the danger that they are so concerned to reconcile past differences that they miss out on the theology of the future, the danger that in the anxiety to attain a visible unity doctrinal questions will be passed over in much too superficial and hasty a manner.

There are other dangers that beset ecumenical theology. One of the most serious is a temptation to use (or misuse) language in such ways that the real issues are blunted or evaded. Ian Henderson went so far as to say that 'ecumenical language is framed not to describe but to conceal',[5] and there is a considerable measure of truth in this complaint. Language is made ambiguous, or terms are made so inclusive that they cease to have any determinable meaning. Let us agree that theological language is never quite precise, and that there is always room for interpretation. Nevertheless, there comes a point at which the language has been so voided of ascertainable content that it does in fact conceal rather than illuminate. Let me give an example. Hans Küng asks: 'What then can "apostolic succession" mean? . . . Who then are the followers of the apostles?' He answers: 'There can only be one basic

33

answer: the church. The whole church, not just a few individuals, is the follower of the apostles.'[6] The statement is true, but it is so obvious as to be utterly jejune. Such language misuse must stultify rather than help ecumenical discussion. It does not help us in the slightest degree to understand, for instance, the significance of the election of Matthias, and in what sense he succeeded to the college of the apostles while the unsuccessful candidate did not (Acts 1.15–26); or what Paul meant when he asked such questions as 'Am I not an apostle?' and 'Are all apostles?' (I Cor. 9.1 and 12.29); or what is to be done about the problem of orders today. The language of ecumenical theology needs to be subjected to strict scrutiny. No doubt the slovenly and misleading usages are unconscious, but their deep-lying motive is probably a desire to arrive at a predetermined result, and such a way of doing theology must be deplored.

Our defence against such dangers must be to remember that in ecumenical theology, as in all theology, truth is established dialectically and dialogically. The truth is not found in a final consensus in which all can rest – and especially not in a consensus so broad or so vague that it is devoid of interest and almost of meaning. Truth is not something at which one arrives, but more of an ongoing process, involving the interplay of different views which sometimes agree, sometimes conflict, sometimes correct each other, but which defy all attempts to subsume them into a single truth. Such a truth would be either a weak compromise or else that fullness of truth which belongs to God alone and in which his creatures will share only at the end of the age. In our present existence, we are on our way to truth, and every theological truth is one that we have in provisional form and is capable of correction.

The fundamental dialectic in ecclesiology and in related questions is the Catholic–Protestant one. This is not to be understood as sheer opposition. Catholicism already contains within itself the possibilities for reformation, while Protestantism carries over elements of catholicity. Catholicism and Protestantism are in some regards opposed, yet neither can do without the other and both represent authentic elements within Christianity. On the other hand, they cannot be collapsed into each other without destroying the fruitfulness of the tension between them.

It is not easy to characterize Catholicism and Protestantism. One of the most suggestive ways of elucidating the distinction is Paul Tillich's contrast between 'Catholic substance' and 'Protestant principle'.[7] The fact that he uses in this connection two different nouns indicates that we are not dealing with two entities of the same order when we contrast Catholicism and Protestantism. Catholicism has to do with the substance, 'the concrete embodiment of the spiritual presence', in Tillich's expression. To put it in another way, the Catholic substance is the given – not a static given, but a given which has its origin in Jesus Christ and has continued to grow and deepen in the church, so that in many matters we can perhaps hardly say with assurance what comes directly from Christ and what has had its origin in the church, though it might well be continuous with, and a natural, even necessary, development from that which was explicit in Christ's own teaching. Catholicism stresses continuity, and the visible historical community as the bearer of that continuity. But now the ambiguity begins to emerge. It can always be asked whether a particular belief or practice is legitimate development or mere accretion; and it can be asked whether the church is arrogating to itself or its officers an authority which belongs only to Christ. It seems to be an extreme form of Catholic ecclesiology that finds expression in Cardinal Newman's famous hymn:

> And I hold in veneration
> For the sake of (Christ) alone
> Holy church as his creation,
> And her teachings as his own.[8]

It is at this point that the Protestant principle will begin to operate. This is a critical principle which seeks to relativize every claim to theological finality or absolute authority. Hence the Protestant insistence on returning to the sources, especially the New Testament, for the criticism of the church. Of course, if the Catholic substance tends to be uncritical and to become authoritarian, the Protestant principle in turn tends to overlook historical development and seeks an illusory primitive faith. This is why Protestantism and Catholicism need each other. They belong together and neither can absorb the other. It is through their dialogue and even conflict that theological advance can be made. This is the way into a broader unifying theological vision that will be based not on the *compromise* of 'consensus theologies' but on the *comprehensiveness* of a theological thinking in which the truth is ever coming to be in a dialectical way.

By way of summary, then, we conclude that while the most important ecumenical theology is simply the endeavours together of theologians from all traditions to give meaningful expression to the great Christian truths for our time, the specifically ecumenical theology of conversation among the traditions concerning their agreements and differences must go on alongside and in the light of fundamental theology. In all theology, both convergences and divergences are necessary if there is to be health and a vigorous growth into the truth. In specifically ecumenical theology, the dynamic is supplied by the tension between Catholic substance and Protestant principle. Each contains elements of the other, and neither is entirely a monopoly of any particular church or group of churches. Neither can do without the other, yet neither can vanquish the other or absorb the other into itself. Their unity consists in their plurality and diversity.

5

Structures of Unity

We must move on now to more concrete and practical problems. How do we envisage the structure of a church at once united and diversified? And can we find more definite theological guidelines than have so far emerged to help us in our task? It is true that a good many theological considerations have already come before us, but they have been of a fairly general nature, as have been also the philosophical and sociological considerations. To be sure, they have all pointed us in the direction of a diversity-in-unity and unity-in-diversity, and we may feel reasonably confident about the direction in which we are moving, but the argument needs to be clinched by a specific theology of the church – an ecclesiology or understanding of the church that would show both unity and diversity as belonging to its essence, and that would therefore carry with it the demand that this should be reflected in its structures.

It must be clear from all that has been said already that the argument is not moving towards a conception of what is usually called 'organic union'. We must notice, of course, that this expression is not very clearly defined. The late Lord Fisher, for instance, used the expression 'organic union' in a fairly broad way for the relation between churches which practise full intercommunion and accord full recognition to each others' ministries. One could then speak of 'organic union' among the autonomous churches of the Anglican communion, or among the autocephalous churches of the East, or, perhaps, between Anglicans and Old Catholics. But usually 'organic union' has had a different sense, and has meant the bringing together into a single church or ecclesial body two or more of the churches operating in a given geographical area, usually a national area; and whatever concessions may be made for a provisional continuation of different traditions, the conception of organic union looks to the goal of a fairly total kind of merger in which existing denominations will be brought into a unified organization, sharing (within permissive limits) the same theology, the same worship, the same administration. It is this second understanding of organic union – the usual understanding of it – that must be contested, because it envisages unity in a way that is too rigid and that must inevitably lead to pressures towards uniformity and the suppression of freedom and diversity. I am well aware, of course, that many eminent ecumenists have maintained that the goal of full organic union is the only one worth pursuing and this view cannot lightly be dismissed. Furthermore, when the pressures of secularization are being felt by all the churches, there are strong practical considerations that drive them in the direction of pooling their resources and streamlining their organization. But I still think that they would be moving in the wrong direction.

It is not only that the conception of organic union is too tight to allow scope for legitimate Christian diversity. A more fundamental defect is that this particular way of conceiving unity has been too exclusively dominated by one particular image of the church, namely, the church as the body of Christ. And with this we are brought at once to face the specifically theological issue: what is the church, and what kind of unity is appropriate to its nature?

I have mentioned a too exclusive concentration on one particular image of the church. There are, of course, many images of the church, some of them as old as the New Testament itself, some derived from later tradition. The church has been represented as the body of Christ, the temple of the Holy Spirit, the bride of Christ, the new people of God and so on, to confine ourselves to the more important biblical images. An image is different from a concept, for it does not try to express the general characteristics of something but rather sets in motion a chain of reflection which is open ended and leads into new insights. Since the church itself is not a merely human phenomenon (or so Christians believe), there belongs to it a depth that cannot be grasped in sociological concepts, though these are certainly applicable to some aspects of the church. This depth is indicated in the images by the expressions 'of Christ', 'of the Holy Spirit' and 'of God'. The bride of Christ is of a different order from the bride of Abydos or the bride of Lammermoor; the temple of the Holy Spirit is not the same kind of temple as the temple of Karnak or the temple in Jerusalem; the people of God has a different kind of peoplehood from the people of France or the people of Wales. The various images help to illuminate and open up the dimension of mystery in the church's being. But because there is an inexhaustibility about this mystery, no single image can by itself be sufficient. Neither can they all be synthesized. They have to be deployed alongside one another, supplementing and even correcting one another.

Nevertheless, it may be the case that at any given time, one image assumes a certain priority, and it may do so because it specially lights up an aspect of the church's being appropriate to the needs and questions of that time. In fact, in the past two or three decades, we have ourselves witnessed a remarkable shift in the priorities of the images of the church. A generation ago, the priority belonged to the image of the church as the body of Christ and to ideas associated with that image, including the idea of organic union. Since the time of Vatican II, however, the priority has passed to another image – the church as the people of God. This image is equally rooted in the Bible and is equally fruitful, but it is different and draws attention to different features of the church's being.

Incidentally, both images strongly support the general position being put forward in this book, namely, that the church is a diversity-in-unity and a unity-in-diversity. The body is a unity, but a unity which consists in and is even enhanced by the great variety of its organs and component parts. A people is likewise a unity, but a unity enriched by the almost infinite variety of those who compose it, a variety extending not only to their functions but to their constitution as persons. But although they have much in common, the two images differ in some important respects. I do not think either of them can be isolated (nor can any of the other classic images of the church). Neither can any of the images be suppressed without loss. Yet I think it has been a right instinct that has led in recent years to a recovery and revitalizing of the image of the people of God, and that this image deserves to enjoy a measure of precedence in our current thinking about the church.

The reason for this judgment can be briefly stated. The image of the people of God is one derived from personal and social being, whereas the image of the body of Christ is a biological image, drawn from the category of organism. To be sure, man has often thought of his personal life in sub-personal analogies – the soul as substance, the self as organism – but it has become increasingly clear that while such ana-logues may have a limited usefulness, the category of personal being is so rich and unique that it cannot be adequately represented in any concepts or images that are themselves less than personal. To think of the church as the people of God is to ensure from the beginning that personal and social categories will be uppermost in our thinking, whereas if we begin from the body of Christ, personal categories tend to be brought in later and never quite overcome the essentially organismic bias of the fundamental image.

Let me mention three ways in which the people of God image introduces into our thinking about the church a flexibility which goes beyond what was possible when the body of Christ image had the ascendancy.

1. When precedence is accorded to the people of God image, the relationships among those who make up the church whether we are thinking of individuals or of ecclesial groups of various kinds, are seen in personal terms, and personal models become dominant in our thinking. Personal and social relations are different from biological relations within an organism, even if there are points of similarity. Personal and social relations are freer and subtler, though at the same time richer. To find out what personal and social relations are, we have to study such models as marriage, friendship, group relations and also political relations. In these latter cases, we

are thinking not simply of the relations between individuals, but still of the human relations of, let us say, different groups in a multi-racial society or different political units in a federal state. Always in healthy personal and social relations there has to be an element of *rapprochement* and an element of distancing, a drawing near to the other and yet an establishing of him in his otherness so that the being that is uniquely his is never absorbed but strengthened. Marriage, for instance, means the intimate union of the partners but also the full flowering of each in his or her unique selfhood. All these personal and social relations have both a freedom and a complexity that cannot be adequately represented by the model of an organism in which the many members are subjected to the unity of the whole.

2. The people of God image has a dynamic quality which further differentiates it from the body of Christ image. To be sure, a body or organism is something alive and therefore dynamic. But its dynamism is contained within its own boundaries. 'Homeostasis' is the technical term which biologists use to describe the unceasing activities of the living organism as it maintains itself in the face of all the pressures of its environment. On the other hand, the dynamic of a people is its history. The notion of history allows for possibilities of choice, of growth, of search, of fulfilment far beyond anything that could be visualized in the case of an organism. The implications for ecumenism are correspondingly important. The union of human groups is not to be accomplished along the lines of homeostasis within an organic or symbiotic relationship, but in the far more dynamic way of growing and deepening personal relationships which will keep on growing and deepening until the final mystery of unity is achieved, and that will be only in the eschatological consummation. Thus it is really absurd to say that the churches became united by such and such a date or will become united by such and such a date. When conceived in personal and social, rather than in organic (and, still less, organizational) terms, the unity of the church is, like its sanctity, something that in history is always coming to be. And every advance in the unity of persons and groups of persons is, paradoxically,

accompanied by the recognition of their differences and uniqueness.

3. A further important difference between our two images is to be noted. A body or biological organism has fairly definite boundaries. These mark it off from its environment, though admittedly there is constant interaction along the boundaries. But a people has much less definite edges, and this is true above all of the people of God. From the founding of the first people of God through the call of Abraham, the boundaries have been blurred and the chosen people tied in many ways to the whole human race; and in the new people of God, the Christian church, the boundaries have been even less clearly drawn so that the church merges into the whole human race, which is ideally the whole people of God on earth. Admittedly, the contrast between the image of the people of God and that of the body of Christ is at this point a relative one, and both of these images stand opposed to the later non-biblical image of the church as the ark of salvation floating upon the stormy waters, for here the separation of church and world seems to have been brought to its sharpest expression. Nevertheless, it is the thought of the people of God standing in solidarity with all people that brings home to us most forcibly the truth that the unity of the church is inseparable from the unity of mankind and cannot rightly be pursued apart from it. The unity of the church, conceived in personal and social terms, is completely open ended, both in time and space.

Further theological light on these questions may be had from a consideration of our Lord's reiterated prayer for the disciples, 'that they may be one' (John 17.11; also 21–2). Rightly, this prayer has been very much in the hearts of those who have espoused the cause of Christian unity. We should be clear, however, that the prayer had nothing to do with what nowadays are called 'schemes' of organic union and relate to situations not envisaged in New Testament times. As Bultmann points out, the unity for which prayer is made here 'is not, of course, thought of as unity of organization'. It cannot be 'manufactured by organization, institutions or dogma; these can at best only bear witness to the real unity, as on the other hand they can also give a false impression of unity'.[1] But what is the 'real unity'? The clue is supplied by the words that follow the prayer: 'that they may be one, *even as we are one*'. The unity is personal unity, and it is personal unity of the most perfect kind, the unity of the Father and the Son. Carrying the argument a step further, it is the unity of the persons of the Trinity. Leaving aside the question of how exactly we are to understand the word 'person' in the context of trinitarian discourse, we can at least say that the divine Triunity represents the ultimate fulfilment of diversity-in-unity and unity-in-diversity and that the imperfect personal and social unities of human life afford some dim prefiguring of that ultimate unity of the Three-in-One.

But now that we have seen the theological background that points us to a form of unity allowing for a maximum of diversity, can we say a little more about the practical structures which such unity-in-diversity might entail? Can we point to any existing structures which exemplify the kind of thing we have in mind?

I believe that the best existing model for Christian unity is that which we find in the relation between the Roman Catholic Church and the so-called 'Uniat' churches of the East. Here I am not concerned with the many ways (some of them decidedly shady) by which these unions were brought about. Neither am I concerned with the actual term 'Uniat' or its anglicized form 'uniate' (in which form I shall use it from now on). But since this term is an ecclesiastical one and has some definite instantiations among the churches, it is useful. Incidentally, it does not mean the same as 'federal'. Not only does the word 'federal' bring along some unwanted political overtones, it is also misleading because it is associated with a loose kind of inter-church association which is quite different from the uniate relation – for instance, federations of Lutheran churches in the United States or of free churches in England. What is of interest is the relation itself, whether we call it 'uniate' or prefer some other name. The uniate relation is one in which there is no attempt to set up a unitary or uniform church, either by absorbing one body into the other or by trying to work out some sort of hybrid. The uniate churches are in full communion with Rome, but retain a measure of autonomy in many areas. They have their own bishops and their own canon law, allowing, for instance, in some cases for married clergy. They have their own liturgies, and their own liturgical languages (even in the days when Latin was universal in the Roman Catholic Church). Furthermore – and this is very important – these churches do not exist only in particular geographical areas but alongside the regular Roman Catholic churches of the Western rite. In other words, the fact that in modern society pluralism is no longer a matter of geography has been frankly recognized. In parts of the United States, for instance, there are both Latin and Uniat bishops with jurisdictions covering the same areas or overlapping areas. Cyprian's famous question, 'Does anyone imagine that there can be in one place many shepherds or several flocks?'[2] demanded a negative answer in the days when societies were homogeneous, but this is no longer the case in the pluralist societies of the contemporary world.

In recent years we have heard of other attempts to establish a uniate style relationship between separated churches, but these have not yet been actualized. In 1963 I first heard Dr A. M. Ramsey discussing the prospects for a union between the Church of England and the Methodists in that country, and he expressly said at that time that the aim was to establish a uniate relation between the two churches. Unfortunately, pressures were exerted demanding the ultimate merger (or 'organic union' in the narrow sense) of the two bodies, and this was one of the reasons for the eventual failure of this whole attempt at union. One would hope, however, for the possible reconsideration of the uniate model, and this possibility should be kept open. We would not have merger but something more valuable, a dynamic and dialectic relationship, described by Douglas Jones as 'the constant cross fertilization of the parish church and the Methodist assemblies, so that a church with a tendency to formalism is constantly held up to the ideals of personal religion and evangelism'.[3] More recently, there has been made in Scotland the suggestion that the Episcopal Church in that country might become a synod of the national Church of Scotland which is, of course, Presbyterian. That church is already composed of a number of synods geographically defined, and the interesting point is that the Episcopal Church would become a non-territorially defined synod, with an area overlapping all the others. This is notable as a breakaway from the dominance of geographical ideas, but the proposal has been deemed premature because there are still considerable theological differences between the two churches that need to be resolved. Nevertheless, this is the kind of pattern that should be further investigated. Finally, it has been hinted by several Roman Catholic spokesmen that if the growing understanding between Rome and Canterbury comes to the point at which some visible unity is possible, this will take the form of a uniate relationship in which the two churches and the two hierarchies will continue side by side in England for an indefinite period.

Such in outline is the uniate model which might well become the goal for the next stage of the ecumenical movement. It would replace the existing denominationalism with a visible unity among the churches, but it would do so in such a way as to continue the rich heritage of varying Christian traditions. It would, moreover, as I have tried to show, accord with a sound theology of the church. The visible unity would find expression not only in the practical forms of ecumenism mentioned in an earlier chapter and not only in the ecumenical tasks of theology but in such common acts of witness and worship as might be deemed appropriate and above all in the full mutual recognition that would be established. Such a form of unity has the further advantage of being open ended. It would be possible for new groups of Christians to join at any time.

Of course, what is envisaged is provisional – as is every historical state of affairs. I have been careful to say that the uniate model might serve the next stage of ecumenism. That next stage might last for a long time – it has even been suggested that a uniate relation between Rome and Canterbury could last for several centuries. What would happen after that? It might be that the two traditions had converged to the extent that nothing would be lost by a total merger.

On the other hand, new and differing traditions might have sprung up. But we need not try to look so far ahead.

These remarks make it clear that I am not saying that a complete merger is always a mistake. Where traditions have almost completely converged, it would seem to be the proper step. But at the present time the main traditions of the Christian church, Roman, Orthodox, Anglican, Lutheran, Reformed, Methodist and others – have an integrity and distinctiveness that ought not to be sacrificed. In the history of religions, syncretism has always proved to be a weakness and there is no reason to suppose that it would be any different in the context of Christian ecumenism. Hybrid national churches and hybrid local congregations become in effect new denominations, but denominations that lack the authenticity of those that have been sculpted in history. We need a way forward that will increase visible unity without decreasing the richness of diversity.

6

Rome the Centre of Unity

In the last chapter there was sketched out in broad strokes the kind of structure that would accord with a church visibly one and yet allowing for the maximum of diversity among its component traditions and individuals – a church taking as its ultimate model the Holy Triunity and one therefore in which there would be neither a dividing of the substance nor a confounding of enriching difference. It would be a church exhibiting the paradox, which we have seen to be theologically well founded, of Christian unity and Christian diversity.

But it was not suggested that the way towards the realization of this goal would be an easy one. To maintain unity and diversity together is much harder than either to impose a hard and fast unity in which differences will be eliminated or to continue in the present state of division. What would be the basic unity needed to reach across the differences and hold them together? How much difference can be maintained without disrupting the unity required for full intercommunication and mutual recognition? Incidentally, there are serious differences in both theology and practice, and I cannot agree with those who would persuade us that the differences among the churches are not important and need not be a barrier to full unity. We shall never attain a unity having any depth if differences are swept under the carpet or treated as matters of no importance. There is all the distance in the world between a comprehensiveness that has seriously faced differences and sought to embrace the very truth expressed in the difference itself, and a vacuousness which, by accepting every point of view, denies any truth claim to all of them.

But what do I mean by 'a comprehensiveness that has seriously faced differences and sought to embrace the very truth expressed in the difference itself'? Let me give an extreme example of the kind of thing I have in mind. Almost all Christians prize the great sacraments of the church. Quakers, however, practise neither baptism nor the eucharist. Is the difference between them and catholic Christians so great that we cannot find a place for them in our concept of Christian unity? Or are we going to say that the difference does not really matter? If we choose the first of these alternatives, we seem to be excluding people who are manifestly Christian. If we choose the second, we are in grave danger of making Christianity so nebulous that it would be left without any distinctive content. But there is a third possibility. Neither the Quaker position nor the majority position on sacraments can be understood in isolation. We have to see them as related within the total Christian history. We then see that Quaker spirituality is a possible development (though an extreme one) of the sacramental principle itself. As J. G. Davies has pointed out, 'Quakers who see all life as sacramental would not have done so without sixteen hundred years of Christian worship.'[1] To say this is to acknowledge that a priority belongs to the traditional Christian sacraments and that these constitute, as it were, a catholic norm. But it is also to acknowledge that, within the total context, Quaker spirituality can find a place. It is within this total context, not independently, that it has meaning, and it has served Christianity as a whole by warning that no particular sacramental system can be absolutized or turned into something merely mechanical and external. Thus, while recognizing that there is a catholic norm, one could also acknowledge that there is a place, perhaps a permanent place, for Quakers within the total context of a Christian diversity-in-unity, though one would see them not so much as a 'uniate church' as rather an autonomous lay religious order, practising a special kind of spirituality.

The background to these remarks is one that was introduced at an earlier stage in this book – the background of Catholic substance and Protestant principle. I said that neither

48

can do without the other and that the exploration of Christian truth takes place in the tension between them. There is on the one hand the given – scriptures, creeds, the stream of tradition including councils, church order and so on. There is on the other hand the constant criticism, questioning, reforming and renewing of the given as each generation appropriates it in the light of its own needs and its own knowledge. The given remains as the norm, that which gives identity and continuity to the church. It provides the comprehensive frame of Christian truth and practice. But it would become fossilized but for the principle of renewal. Any concept of church unity must take account of both aspects. Those who are determined to preserve the given quite unaltered even to the very words in which it has been expressed have made unity virtually impossible. Likewise, those who think they can make up the Christian faith as though they were starting from scratch and nothing binding had come to them from the church's past have ruled out the possibility of unity. Only when Catholic substance and Protestant principle are held together and the critique takes place within the framework of the given is a true unity-in-diversity possible.

But can we define the given, the catholic norms, with both such definiteness and such flexibility that it can be a useful conception? Actually, as we noted early in this book, agreement on the given is much more extensive and solid than we often realize, because we so often concentrate on controversial issues that may not be quite central. The canon of scripture, the catholic creeds, the dominical sacraments, even the threefold ministry are so widely accepted and have so long a history that they constitute something like a normative given. They have in fact provided the content for the Chicago–Lambeth Quadrilateral, and wherever serious ecumenical discussions are going on nowadays, something like the Quadrilateral seems to be assumed. But it might be worth considering whether, instead of working with an abstract idea of the framework of unity, we thought rather in terms of the historic churches and groups that are involved. What is aimed at is not an abstract principle of unity but the living visible unity of the churches themselves – a personal and social unity, as I suggested in the last chapter. So I am going to claim that the centre around which Christian unity is to be built up is not a formula but – at least, so far as the West is concerned – Rome. The separated churches of the West are the estranged daughters (or, in some cases, grand-daughters) of Rome. The Roman Catholic Church is, for us in the West, the bearer in a special way of the Catholic substance and is for this reason at the centre of the movement towards unity.

Of course, this does not necessarily mean a privileged position for Rome – it could mean equally well a special role of responsibility. The American New Testament scholar, John Knox, put the matter very well:

The major split in the Christianity of the West is obviously the separation between Rome and the other denominations, and the ultimate healing of the division in the Western church involves, above all other separations, this primary and basic rift. This rift can be overcome, it seems to me, only through what one can hardly avoid calling a 'return' – not, I hasten to add, that the whole responsibility for Christian reunion in the West rests with the Anglicans and Protestants. Rome, too, must make a 'return' to the more ancient standards of church life represented by scripture and the earliest traditions, reaching a ground not only for possible union in the West, but for reunion with Eastern Orthodoxy as well. The 'return' we are contemplating is not so much the return of one body to another as a turning by all of us together to the apostolic and early catholic sources and norms of the church's life as a historic community. For, although the united church we hope for belongs to the future and will represent a fresh, creative work of the Spirit, it will not be a new church; it will be the historical church in its unmistakable identity, realizing more fully its true nature and destiny.[2]

Knox's remarks arose in the course of an article in which he was expressing his doubts about an American move (the Consultation on Church Union) to promote the merger into a united church of almost a dozen denominations. His doubt was whether such a union, with the Roman Catholic Church left out, would really forward the cause of unity or would in the long run hinder it. This doubt seemed to be confirmed later by the comments of G. H. Tavard, a Roman Catholic observer at the Consultation, who claimed that its underlying ecclesiology, as revealed in its goal of a national institutional merger, was very far removed from a Catholic ecclesiology.[3] But to return for a moment to Knox, we find him saying:

> Anglicans and Protestants cannot make the 'return' (to unity) by by-passing the Roman Catholic Church. There is no possible detour or shortcut. The Roman Church lies squarely and massively in the way we must travel. We can make the 'return' only as the Roman Church makes it too, so that we make it together. There are many signs that such a return is beginning to take place within the Roman Church and that, correspondingly, it is becoming more open to those whom it is calling the 'separated brethren'. This new openness on the part of Rome . . . is the major, the miraculous, the incomparably significant ecumenical fact of our time.[4]

I agree very much with this judgment.

Let us remember, however, that neither 'Catholic substance' nor 'Protestant principle' belongs exclusively to any one church. All Christian churches and denominations share to some extent in the Catholic substance, the given. On the other hand, the Roman Catholic Church has made it very clear in recent years that it contains within itself those resources for self-criticism and renewal that may fairly be called the 'Protestant principle'. When this is said, however, it remains true that the Roman Catholic Church is, in a unique way, the guardian of catholicity. Rome claims to have the fullness of the catholic faith, and even if this claim is controversial, one cannot deny the further claim that, of all Christian communions, the Roman communion is the most truly international and worldwide. Local, regional or national mergers of non-Roman Christian bodies can hardly be more than denominational realignments, or even new denominations. That is why it is so important for Rome to be involved in movements towards unity and why we must see Rome as the centre of unity.

But here we come up against a question, the answer to which seems to me to be not yet clear. How far is Rome prepared to become involved in movements towards greater visible unity and to become a centre drawing all Christians into a new fellowship? Certainly, John Knox is right in stressing that the dramatic ecumenical advances in Roman Catholic thinking since Vatican II constitute the incomparably significant development in ecumenism today. Certainly, too, the many agreements reached in conversations between Roman Catholics on the one side and various non-Roman communions on the other have been very important. Certainly one must allow time for proper consideration if a true and lasting unity is to be achieved – and in this connection, it is worth recalling some wise words of Ian Henderson: 'Ecumenism needs analysis and criticism, rather than haste.'[5] Nevertheless, one can hardly help asking to what extent the Roman Catholic Church is willing not only to observe and to advise but to become itself the centre of unity and give leadership.

Some years ago my friend Hans Küng asked me to contribute to the journal *Concilium* an article on the theme, 'What still separates us from the Catholic Church?' This was to be an Anglican response, and he had commissioned similar responses from Lutheran and Orthodox theologians. I began my article by warning the readers that because of the great diversity of views within Anglicanism I could not pretend that my response would be representative of the Anglican communion as a whole. But I continued: 'Nevertheless, I think that a great many Anglicans, even an overwhelming majority of them, will agree with me if I first of all answer the question, "What still separates us from the Catholic Church?" by saying that, in a very real and important sense, *nothing separates us from the Catholic Church*. Anglicanism has never considered itself to be a sect or denomination originating in the sixteenth century. It continues without a break the *Ecclesia Anglicana* founded by St Augustine thirteen centuries ago, though nowadays this branch of the church has spread far beyond the boundaries of England.'[6] Not only Anglicans, but all Christians, claim to participate to some degree in catholicity – though the expression 'to some degree' is not entirely satisfactory, since it is not a quantitative matter. We could not, for instance, say that Rome is 100% catholic, Lutherans 70%, Baptists 50% and so on – this would be manifestly absurd. As the Orthodox theologian Georges Florovsky has said; 'The catholicity of the church is not a quantitative or a geographical expression . . . it means first of all the inner wholeness and integrity of the church's life.'[7] But although catholicity is not something quantifiable, one may acknowledge that there are certain signs of catholicity, and that these may be more or less manifested in particular churches. I think too that Anglicans and others would be ready to acknowledge that their catholicity would be deepened and enhanced through a closer relation to Rome, considered as the centre.

But all this suggests that one has to put a counter-question to the question posed in *Concilium*. This counter-question is addressed to Rome, and it would run somewhat as follows: 'What form of catholicity would the separated churches need to manifest so that Rome could take them into a unifying relationship and so that they could then advance together into a deeper catholicity?' Or, to put the question in more definite terms, related to an earlier part of the discussion: 'How deep or how extensive an agreement on catholic essentials would Rome need to find in Orthodox, Anglicans, Lutherans, Reformed or whatever group it might be, in order to take them into a uniate relationship of intercommunion and mutual recognition?' If there could be some fairly clear answer to this question, then I think it would also define a clear goal for the movement towards unity and give great impetus to the movement. Rome would definitely emerge as the focus and centre of the movement, which has tended to be very diffuse when local and national *rapprochements* between denominations have taken up so much time and attention. Perhaps, of course, we are being too impatient in pressing such a question at this stage. Perhaps we must wait until there has been much more preliminary spadework in the way of conversations between the Roman Catholic Church and other churches. One must acknowledge, for instance, that the agreed statements on the eucharist and on ministry reached by the Anglican–Roman Catholic International Commission have been documents of great significance and inspire considerable hope for the future. But one would also like to know what can be hoped for after such conversations, assuming that they do uncover a broad basis of agreement within which differences can be contained. May we reasonably hope that some kind of uniate relationship, an extension of that which already is found in the Roman communion, will be set up, with Rome at the centre and other groups related to Rome and to one another in such a way that the visible unity of the church will be more fully manifested than at present, yet the diverse riches of the several heritages will be preserved? Individual Roman Catholic theologians have, of course, been thinking along these lines. The Jesuit Edward P. Echlin is far from being alone when he writes: 'Since Vatican II there has been a development towards pluralism in the Church of Rome. The uniformity promoted before the council is yielding to a comprehensiveness that augurs well for the convergence of Christian churches. When Rome embraces her sister churches in full communion, it seems certain that these churches will be, in the celebrated phrase of Malines, "united, not absorbed". Such unity – in a coexistence in full communion – will be a preliminary step leading to even wider unity and catholicity.'[8] Cardinal Willebrands has also commended the uniate model under the name of a 'typology of churches', and he argues, as I have done in earlier parts of this book, that the virtue of such an arrangement is that it will allow the gospel to reach in different ways the many different kinds of human beings: 'If a typology of churches, a diversity-in-unity and unity-in-diversity, multiplies the possibilities of identifying and celebrating the presence of God in the world; if it brings nearer the hope of providing an imaginative framework within which Christian witness can transform human consciousness for today, then it has all the justification it needs.'[9]

In most of what follows in this book, I shall be seeking to find a way towards the basis for unity on the 'uniate' or 'typology of churches' model. I shall do this by taking up a number of questions on which there is experienced a tension between 'Catholic substance' and 'Protestant principle', and I shall try to suggest ways towards solutions that will rest not on compromise but on the effort to comprehend mutually corrective truths. Of course, I can deal with only a mere fraction of the problems, but if we can succeed with some, there is hope of succeeding with the others.

These chapters on the 'disputed questions' may be considered both an olive branch to Rome and yet a challenge. They are an olive branch, because I am striving to make the full Catholic substance the framework for an understanding of the questions. But they are also a challenge in the sense that they are questions addressed to Rome – questions concerning how much diversity Rome is prepared to allow within the unifying framework, and whether the kind of things said here come anywhere within sight of providing a theological basis for 'unity without absorption' between Rome and the separated churches, and among these separated churches themselves.

7

Quaestiones Disputatae:

1 Ministry

Among the disputed questions on which we shall try to see a way through to a comprehensive solution, embracing both Catholic substance and the operation of Protestant principle, we shall consider first the ordained ministry. This may not be the most central problem in ecumenical discussion, but it has proved to be one of the most stubborn. Bishop Kirk wrote:

> As plans and conferences with unity as their goal have successively cleared the issues involved, it has become generally recognized that the crux of the whole matter is the doctrine of the ministry. Is the ministry from above or from below? Is it a gift to the church from her Saviour and Founder, or an expedient evolved by the church to meet the exigencies of her daily life? Has it a commission transmitted in orderly sequence from the Lord himself, or is it commissioned simply and solely by the congregation of believers among whom the minister is to serve?[1]

These are questions that go to the heart of the matter and they must be faced if we are ever to arrive at the visible sacramental unity envisaged in the earlier parts of this book. There are, of course, other difficult problems relating to the sacraments, to creeds and to other matters, some of which we shall consider in subsequent chapters. But Bishop Kirk was right in seeing that the ministry is somehow a crux. Over the centuries there have grown up two rather sharply distinguished ways of thinking of the ordained ministry. The Catholic view has stressed the continuity of ministry as a visible, personal, historical succession, which is traced back through the bishops as the bearers of this succession to the earliest ministry of the church and, ideally, to the apostles;

it has stressed the sacramental aspects of ministry, and associated ministry chiefly with the eucharist; it has recognized orders of ministry, especially the classic threefold ordering of bishops, priests and deacons; it has stressed that ministry is conferred by Christ and has believed that it consists not only in certain functions but in a status within the church. The Protestant view, on the contrary, has not hesitated to speak of discontinuity in the ministry, when the Protestant principle of renewal seemed to call for a critique of the established order; it has stressed faithfulness to apostolic truth as the link which relates it to Christ and the apostles and has not usually claimed to stand in the kind of historic succession prized by the Catholic view; it has tended to see the preaching of the word as the main function of ministry; it usually adheres to a doctrine of the parity of all ministers; in some cases, though not in all, the Protestant view considers the ordained ministry to be conferred by the congregation as an extension of the general ministry of the people of God, and so to be purely functional.

I have stated the opposition in very summary form, but I do not think I have exaggerated. In this matter, the conflict between Catholic substance and Protestant principle seems specially acute, perhaps because the two have been allowed to drift apart and are not seen within the total Christian context.

However, I think that recent theological thinking on the ministry has made the whole approach to this problem much more hopeful than it was even a generation ago. Instead of two utterly opposed views of the ministry, we can at least begin to see the two points of view as standing in that dialectical type of relation which is characteristic of the Catholic–Protestant tension in theology. Let me pass in review five points concerning ministry and priesthood, all relevant to contemporary ecumenical discussion.

1. All Christian ministry is derived from Christ, and all Christian priesthood is participation in his one priesthood. He is the mediator between God and man, the great High Priest who sums up in himself all priesthood. This understanding of Christ finds, as we all know, its classic expression in the Epistle to the Hebrews. The old type of priesthood and its cultic practices have been superseded and taken up into the

eternal priesthood of Christ, who is both the one sufficient priest and the one sufficient victim. In calling into being his church and in entrusting to it the continuation of his mission on earth, Christ has granted to the church a participation in his priestly ministry, a share in his priesthood. This participation is granted in various ways – I purposely avoid saying 'degrees' – for the church is not a homogeneous mass but a true people of God with all the differentiation of function and identity that belong to a people. Within this people, there are different forms of ministry and priesthood. They are distinct in the economy of the church, yet they are all related and interdependent and have their being in the context of the church as a whole. This means that no one of them can, so to speak, 'go it alone'. This is collegiality in the broadest sense, and it is founded on the fact that all ministry and priesthood derive from the sole priesthood of Christ.

2. Among the forms of priesthood, we acknowledge first a priesthood of the whole church, a priesthood in which all share in virtue of their membership in the people of God. The church is 'a royal priesthood, God's own people' (I Pet. 2.9). This priesthood of the whole people of God, though it has been overshadowed in times of clericalism, is fundamental. Other priesthood cannot be separated from it. It was clearly taught in the New Testament, it was reasserted by Luther and other Reformers, and it is being stressed again today. Only a lively apostolate of the laity can carry the Christian mission into the secularized society of our time. We must recognize that baptism is itself a kind of ordination. The laity is by far the largest order in the church, and it shares with the other orders the fundamental ministry entrusted to us all – the 'ministry of reconciliation' (II Cor. 5.18–20). All other ministry is for the sake of this fundamental ministry by which God, first through the incarnate Lord and then through the Lord in his church, is reconciling the world to himself. Let us note that the most important ministry of the laity is a secular informal ministry, fulfilling itself in daily life. To symbolize their participation in the priestly action of the whole church, the lay people have also their definite and inalienable part in the liturgy. But this liturgical ministry of the laity is secondary to

58

ministry in the world, and must not be allowed to obscure it. We make a serious mistake if we try to turn the layman's ministry into an imitation of the ministry of the cleric, and we detract from the true worth and dignity of the lay ministry.

3. Another form of ministry has a more definitely liturgical and sacramental character. This is the priesthood or *sacerdotium* of the ordained ministry, more precisely, the priesthood which bishops share with presbyters. They all participate in the general priesthood of the whole church, in the ministry of reconciliation. But they are also charged with a special ministry of word and sacraments. There is no conflict between these two forms of priesthood. On the contrary, as R. C. Moberly argued, 'the priesthood of the ministry is to be established not through depreciation but through exaltation of the priesthood of the whole body'.[2] The duty of those having a special ministry is, among other things, to nurture the whole people of God for the exercise of the royal priesthood that belongs to all. In this sense, special ministry is for the sake of the general ministry. It follows also that bishops and presbyters are not highly privileged persons within the church, but the servants of the whole people, with special responsibilities.

While I have stressed the relation of this special priesthood to the general priesthood, we must be clear too about its distinctness. It is not just a specialized function within the general priesthood, a function for which some people are set apart by their fellows in order to represent them. When we talk of ordination and holy orders, we are implying that within the people, there are orders. From the beginning, the church was no amorphous entity but a structured people with a co-ordinated life. As Moberly remarks, 'the church without apostolate never existed for a moment'. But equally, the apostolate never existed or could have existed for a moment without the church.

The differentiated nature of priesthood within the church is just as clearly evident from the New Testament as is the general priesthood of the whole people, for the gospels make it clear that the apostles had a distinctive ministry in the church. They derived this directly from Christ (or so the New Testament writers believed) and it was not delegated to them by their fellow Christians. But we return to the point that the apostles received their ministry within the context of the church. The Catholic–Protestant tension generated by the question whether the ministry is from above or below, whether the apostles founded the church or the church generated the ministry, is a false disjunction. The truth is the more complex one that from the beginning the Christian church was an ordered people. Its order is constitutive, and so equiprimordial with its existence. To recognize this point is to bypass many of the sterile disputes of the past.

The distinctive ministry, first exercised by the apostles, was continued by their successors. We do not know the historical details of the early period and doubtless the New Testament account of the early ministry is itself already idealized, but it is a doctrinal rather than a historical meaning that is intended when the 'Decree on the Ministry and Life of Priests' of Vatican II summarizes the matter thus: 'Christ sent the apostles, just as he himself had been sent by the Father; through these same apostles he made their successors, the bishops, sharers in his consecration and mission. Their ministerial role has been handed down to priests in a limited degree.'[3]

The precise functions of these early ministers is not entirely known. Preaching, baptizing, healing, caring for the churches, performing acts that resemble ordination and confirmation – we have evidence of all of these. But in course of time it came about that the distinct *sacerdotium* of the bishop (and presbyter) was his presidency at the eucharist, and so it remains to this day. Because the priesthood of bishops and presbyters has this eucharistic character, Roman Catholic theologians used to make much of the idea of a 'sacrificing' priesthood. This notion was prominent, for instance, in the deliberations which led to the unhappy condemnation of Anglican orders in 1896. But more recent Catholic theology has moved towards a broader conception of priesthood. Just as the meaning of the eucharist itself is not exhausted by the concept of sacrifice (though this is certainly one constituent) so priesthood cannot be tied exclusively to sacrifice. For this reason, I should think that the concept of priesthood, as now understood by many

Roman Catholic theologians, would be much less objectionable to Protestants than the older emphasis on 'sacrificing' priesthood.

Before moving to the next point, let me say something about the ambiguity in the words 'priest' and 'priesthood'. They are used to refer not only to the *sacerdotium* which we have just been discussing but also to refer to the presbyterate (*presbyteratus*) or second order of the traditional threefold ministry. Strictly speaking, the fullness of priesthood and ministry belongs to the bishops. As the Dutch Catechism says, 'the fullness of pastoral power and authority is given to the bishops – they are *the* priests of the church'.[4] But in the parishes, all the essential priestly functions are carried out by presbyters, and so, in popular usage, 'priest' commonly means 'presbyter'. This can cause confusion, and in theological discussions about the ministry, it is helpful to talk of 'presbyters' when we are referring to the second order of the ministry. This is in no sense to deny their *sacerdotium*, and the practice is to be advocated more for the sake of clarity than for the sake of placating those who dislike the word 'priest'. For myself, I hope that in everyday language the term 'priest' will continue to be used as in the past. The words 'priest' and 'presbyter' are cognate. We may recall Milton's famous objection to presbyterianism: ' "Presbyter" is but "priest" writ large.' It says the same thing in a more long-winded way. The Christian presbyter is a priest, both in his sharing of the priesthood of the whole church and in his sharing of the special priesthood of the bishop. In Moberly's words, 'it would be a superficial and wrong following of scripture to strike out the words "priest", "priesthood", "sacrifice".'[5]

4. A further important development in current thinking on these questions holds out great hope. Because of the recognition that the forms of ministry and priesthood are varied and differentiated, theological discussion has moved away from the 'all or nothing' attitudes of earlier debates. It was that attitude which made some of these debates so embittered. It was taken that either you were a priest or you were not, either you had the fullness of ministry or you had none at all, either your orders were valid or they were

invalid. We see now that such disjunctions were too simplistic by far. There are many forms of ministry, and many modes of participation in ministry and priesthood. Wherever there comes about reconciliation in the spirit of Christ through some human agency, there we have effective Christian ministry. Certainly, we can talk about the classic form of the ministry, and I would certainly want to uphold this form. But one need not for a moment deny that wherever Christ works through his servants, he is conferring on them a share in his ministry and priesthood.

5. The last point I want to make is this: there is no *single* criterion for the apostolic ministry. In the past, great stress has been laid by Roman Catholic and Anglican theologians on one particular constitutive element in this ministry, namely, its transmission through the succession of bishops, a transmission symbolized by the laying on of hands. This is undoubtedly a part of the fullness of the ministry, and an important part. But it is not the whole, or the only element in apostolic succession. Equally important is the transmission of the apostolic truth. In some cases, this apostolic teaching in its essentials continues, even where episcopal succession was lost; and in such cases, one cannot deny an important continuity with the apostles. On the other hand, if one were to visualize the continuity only in terms of an external and mechanical tactual succession without regard to apostolic truth – though admittedly we are here considering a caricature rather than an actually existing state of affairs – then one would need to raise questions as to whether this constituted a genuine continuity with the apostles. In either extreme case, one would have a broken ministry.

Protestants have tended to emphasize the apostolic preaching as the essential which must be maintained in a true Christian ministry. They have been right to assert this as against any merely mechanical or magical ideas of ministry, and to this extent we have a proper exercise of the Protestant principle. But to lay all the stress on truth and teaching is to run the risk of a gnostic type of theology. Catholics have been right on their side in emphasizing the historical, incarnate nature of the church. The true church is not, as Calvin supposed, an invisible church. It exists in history and stands in physical continuity with the church of all ages, with the apostles and with the incarnate Lord himself. Once again, we find that what might once have seemed an intractable difference between Catholic and Protestant ways of thinking can be to some extent resolved in a broader context. The new outlook is well expressed in a balanced statement coming from the World Council of Churches' Secretariat on Faith and Order:

> Churches which have preserved the episcopal succession have to recognize the real content of the ordained ministry that exists in churches that do not have such an episcopal succession. . . . The churches without episcopal succession have to recognize that, while they may not lack a succession in apostolic faith, they do not have the fulness of the *sign* of apostolic succession. If full visible unity is to be achieved, the fulness of the sign of apostolic succession ought to be recovered.[6]

In the five points enumerated above, I have tried to set forth an understanding of ministry widely accepted today, one that is based on the Catholic substance but which recognizes the valid thrusts of Protestant principle. What practical steps might follow that would lead towards our goal of a visible unity-in-diversity?

Some years ago I made the suggestion that we might explore the possibility of a common ordinal.[7] As more and more groups might be persuaded to use it, then there would gradually grow up a ministry universally recognized, though differentiated according to the customs of the various churches. Such an ordinal, I assumed, would provide for episcopal ordination, and one might hope that Roman Catholic bishops would eventually take part in the ordinations, so giving them a claim to wide recognition. In this way, the ordinal would be based on the Catholic substance of the doctrine of the ministry. But it would also incorporate whatever might seem of value in the Protestant principle, as applied to that doctrine.

When I first commended this idea, no appropriate ordinal was available. But in 1968 there was published by the Commission on Anglican–Methodist Unity an ordinal which seems to me to be precisely the kind of thing needed. The fact that the Anglican–Methodist scheme came to nothing should not lead us to overlook the more important fact that it produced a major theological and ecumenical document in the proposed ordinal. I believe this ordinal could still be used to build the unity of the future. It could be very helpful in many situations beyond the one which its authors originally envisaged. Indeed, the wide use and acceptance of this ordinal (or one like it) could lead to a major ecumenical breakthrough all over the world.

This new ordinal was really new, not just a revision of the existing Anglican and Methodist ordinals or an attempt at conflation. It has been based on careful scholarly study of the origins and development of the ordained ministry, and its claim to be ecumenical rests on the fact that not only the two churches directly involved had a hand in it, but Roman Catholic, Orthodox and Protestant scholars were all consulted. The Roman Catholic ordinals have themselves been undergoing revision and simplification, and eminent Roman Catholic scholars have indicated that, in their opinion, the new ordinal meets all the criteria relating to the Roman Catholic understanding of ordination.

It contains three services: 'The Ordination of Deacons', 'The Ordination of Presbyters, also called Priests' and 'The Ordination or Consecration of Bishops'. There is also a preface which spells out some of the implications underlying the rites. The great merit of the book is that, like the theology of ministry expounded in the first part of this chapter, it does not seek a compromise but seeks rather to hold together the different elements in the tradition within an embracing unity which does not infringe their integrity. In particular, it does this with the doctrines of general ministry and special ministry. They are both fully recognized in their integrity, without confusion or absorption, yet without separation.

Perhaps I am wrong in suggesting the use of a common ordinal (which I would visualize as being used among the separated churches of the West) and it would be more in accord with our stress on diversity to allow for a variety of ordinals, each of which might stress some aspects of ministry and leave others latent. This may be so, but clearly in this matter of ordination there needs to be a common basis, more perhaps than in some of the other matters we have to consider, if there is to be the desired mutual recognition. What would be needed to move towards a uniate relation in ministry between Rome and the other churches of the West? Under what conditions would Roman bishops be willing to take part in consecrations and ordinations? One would like to have some guidance from Rome on these matters.

What is contemplated here is not, of course, 'instant union' (an impossibility in any case) but a growing together which would take a generation or more and at the end of that time would have brought us to the stage of the uniate relation. The process might be supplemented by a service of reconciliation of existing ministries, as was also visualized in the Anglican–Methodist proposals. All ministries, after all, have some defects so long as the sacramental unity of the church is incomplete. If it is true that we all in various ways have a share in ministry and priesthood, it is true that we all lack something of its fullness – even, one may say, the Pope and the Archbishop of Canterbury. For if the end of all ministry is reconciliation, our ministries are imperfect so long as they are unreconciled. And perhaps it is the need for visible reconciliation rather than supplementing the process of growing together in ministry that points to the desirability of some overt sacramental act of reconciliation among existing ministries.

8

Quaestiones Disputatae:

2 Eucharist

Eucharistic doctrine and practice have been traditionally one of the most divisive areas among Christians, and especially between Catholics and Protestants. But today we are moving towards a more comprehensive view of the eucharist, and within it some of the differences can be seen as differences of emphasis.[1] There are many aspects of meaning packed into the eucharist – memorial, sacrifice, presence, common meal, thanksgiving and so on. It is entirely right that in certain traditions or at certain periods one aspect has been specially stressed. But it is wrong when one aspect is stressed to the exclusion of others, and this has sometimes happened.

I shall not attempt here a general discussion of modern eucharistic theology but will take up some of the most delicate and controversial issues, namely, those relating to real presence, reservation, devotion to Christ in the sacrament reserved, and the doctrine of transubstantiation. It was noted by many commentators that the Anglican–Roman Catholic agreed statement on the eucharist avoided mention of reservation and eucharistic devotions, and relegated transubstantiation to a footnote. I shall try to show, however, that on the basis of the eucharistic theology briefly expressed in that document, and on the basis of other possible theologies, there is no problem about belief in a real abiding presence of Christ in the eucharist. It is this belief that makes possible the wealth of eucharistic spirituality in the Roman Catholic Church (as also among many Anglicans and Lutherans), but since these devotions have always been regarded as optional, their absence among Christians who might share essentially the same theology of the eucharist is not indicative of an insuperable division between the two groups. Once again, we may be able to see the difference as the tension between Catholic substance and Protestant principle within the totality of Christian truth.

It is often said that the primary purpose in the reservation or retention of the consecrated elements of the eucharist is to allow for the communion of the sick and unavoidably absent, and this is unquestionably so. Nowadays many Protestant and evangelical Christians would find no great difficulty in retaining some of the consecrated elements for the purpose of taking them to the sick after the public service. But it is doubtful whether this was ever the *sole* purpose of reservation, and in fact the taking of communion to the sick cannot be rigidly isolated from other practices associated with reservation, including prayers and devotional practices responding to the eucharistic presence of Christ.

That reservation has always served more than one purpose may be seen from a glance at the history of the practice. Writing in the middle of the second century, Justin simply mentions that the deacons carry away some of the eucharistic bread 'to those that are absent'.[2] We usually assume that the sick are intended, but there could have been many reasons for absence in those days – some might be slaves who could not get away from work, others might be in prison, and so on. Also, there is no indication of how much time might elapse before it was possible for those absent to receive the gifts reserved for them. It is unlikely that it would always be possible to carry the gifts directly to them after the eucharist, though this might be the ideal.

We have to broaden our understanding of reservation still further when we consider the practice, widespread in the second and third centuries, of retaining the sacrament in the homes and even, for security, on the persons of the faithful, in order that they might communicate themselves from it frequently, possibly daily. Tertullian mentions the Christian wife of a pagan husband who made a practice of taking the sacrament secretly at home before her ordinary food,[3] and there are many other mentions of a similar kind. Here then we have a form of reservation which was not for the sick or for emergencies but for the sake of frequent communion.

The usual explanation, which seems plausible enough, is that because of the dangers of persecution, celebrations of the eucharist could not be frequent, and so the desire for frequent communion could be met only through reserving the sacrament in the people's homes. It would, of course, be generally agreed that ideally Christians ought to make their communions in company with their fellow believers and in the course of a full eucharistic liturgy. But conditions are not always ideal. Dom Gregory Dix has remarked: 'I doubt if it has been generally recognized that owing to the absence of a daily celebration of the eucharist, at all events as a normal practice, and the prevalance on the other hand of daily communion, the actual majority (numerically speaking) of acts of communion during the third century must have been made quite apart from any celebration of the liturgy, by means of the reserved sacrament.'[4]

An interesting parallel may be cited from more recent times. In Scotland, the Penal Laws, in force from 1746 to 1792, forbade the assembling together of more than eight episcopalians in one place – and this at a time when episcopalians were (relatively speaking) much more numerous in Scotland than they are today. The only feasible practice was to hold small celebrations and to communicate the bulk of the people from the reserved sacrament. In the Scottish church, reservation is, in the words of a rubric in the liturgy, a 'long existing custom'.

Still further considerations are raised by the ancient use of the *fermentum*. In accordance with this custom, which seems to have been first mentioned by Irenaeus near the end of the second century,[5] part of the consecrated bread was carried away from the eucharist not for the sick but to presbyters celebrating in local churches, apparently as a sign that there is one church and one eucharist and perhaps also as a symbol of the bishop's jurisdiction. It was a unity both in time and space, for at a later period some of the consecrated bread was not only carried from the bishop's eucharist to other churches, but some was kept from one celebration to another in the mother church, thereby stressing the continuity of the eucharist.[6]

Enough has been said to show that the reservation or retention of the consecrated elements could have several ends in view, though obviously some have been more important than others. Let me now say something more specific about the function of the reserved sacrament as a centre of devotion.

Reverence for the consecrated elements begins within the consecrated liturgy itself where, not in isolation but in the total context of the people making eucharist, the consecrated bread and wine became the focal point of Christ's presence. Michael Moreton has drawn attention to the reverential expressions used for the consecrated elements in early liturgies – phrases such as *sancta tua, mensa coelestis, mysteria veneranda, coelestia dona, munera divina*, etc.[7] If these elements were carried out of the immediate context of the eucharist, they were still the subject of reverence. For instance, the *Apostolic Tradition* gives instructions about the keeping of the sacrament at home (the practice mentioned above) and makes it clear that the eucharistic bread is to be treated with the greatest reverence – it must not be allowed to fall, it must not get lost, it must be protected against the depredations of mice![8] If the eucharistic bread is retained for communion, it is only natural that this should be done with reverence, and it is natural also that this initial reverence might develop into more definite forms of devotion. The close link between taking the sacrament to the sick and devotional practices is strikingly illustrated by the fact that the Corpus Christi procession, perhaps the most flamboyant of all extra-liturgical devotions, had a very simple origin in the carrying of the viaticum to the sick.[9] Indeed, the whole phenomenon of reservation and the practices that came to be associated with it are to be understood in terms of the extension of the original eucharistic context. Edward Schillebeeckx writes: 'The words of the new covenant are pronounced over this bread, and Christ's offer of grace remains real in it so long as it remains a sign . . . reservation is so surrounded by reverence that the eucharistic context is clearly preserved.'[10]

No doubt the great upsurge of eucharistic devotion in the

thirteenth century placed a whole new emphasis on the devotional aspects of reservation – as also on the veneration of the elements within the eucharist itself – but this was a development, even if an exaggerated one, of practices and attitudes that had been growing for a very long time and had existed in some form from the earliest times. One sometimes hears it said that it was the acceptance of the doctrine of transubstantiation by the Lateran Council in 1215 that led to the eucharistic developments of the thirteenth century, but this is erroneous and puts the cart before the horse. The relation of the *lex orandi* to the *lex credendi* is always a reciprocal one, and the doctrine of transubstantiation was quite as much a rationalizing of earlier belief and practice as a stimulus to later development. 'Even though the particular doctrine of transubstantiation belongs to a later period,' writes Maurice Wiles, 'yet its essential spirit was fully developed within the patristic age.'[11]

On the practical side, the elevation of the host after the words of institution has sometimes been seen as indicative of a new attitude. Interestingly enough, this practice antedates the official adoption of transubstantiation by at least a few years – Jungmann places its introduction around 1210.[12] But it is very important to remember that what was new at the beginning of the thirteenth century was not the elevation of the consecrated elements in itself, but the practice of having separate elevations of the host and the chalice immediately following the words of institution, and so introducing a dramatic moment of consecration. The elevation of the elements was itself far from new – it had been described more than five hundred years earlier and it may have been done for a long time before anyone thought of describing it. According to *Ordo Romanus Primus* (usually dated about 700) the host and chalice were elevated together at the doxology ending the great prayer. The bishop lifted up the *oblata* while the deacon raised the chalice. Theologically, this was a much sounder practice than the separate elevations, for it recognized that the whole prayer is the prayer of consecration. This primitive elevation survived as the so-called 'little elevation', but liturgical reformers are now seeking to restore its primacy.

Up to this point, the argument has had a twofold aim. I have tried to show that devotion to Christ under the sacramental species begins with the eucharist itself, and is carried over if the elements are taken out of the immediate context of the eucharistic liturgy; though it is important to note that they remain within the wider context of the eucharistic community, for the reserved elements are not separated from the eucharist (this would be nonsense!) but rather the eucharistic context is extended. I have also tried to show that reservation for the sick cannot be isolated and includes latent possibilities for devotion. For the sacrament cannot be retained or reserved in a merely casual way, as if one could be resolved to take a precious gift to the sick and yet be also resolved to treat that gift lightly. The sacrament is reverently retained just as it is reverently consumed, and this reverential attitude may properly issue in some kind of prayer and devotion. If the sacrament is reserved in a particular place, many people find it very natural and helpful to pray there.

The latent possibilities for devotion in a theology which may not have made any explicit mention of these possibilities has been made clear by Bishop Butler. Writing in *The Times* of 15 September 1971, Bishop Butler commented on the 'substantial' agreement on the eucharist reached by Anglican and Roman Catholic theologians, and he asked: 'Apart from the word "transubstantiation", is there any significant area in which the commission's substantial agreement in fact falls short of full agreement?' He tells us he can think of only one possible disagreement. It arises from the fact that 'we Catholics of the Western Rite have now for centuries drawn devotional conclusions from the doctrine of the real presence, and have expressed our adoration of the body and blood of Christ not only in the course of the eucharist itself (as at the elevation of the host immediately after the words of institution of the sacrament) but after the mass is over, in, for instance, the service of benediction, and by genuflecting when passing in front of the blessed sacrament reserved in tabernacle or aumbry.' The commission's silence on these matters led him to wonder 'whether there is not actually some doctrinal point here which needs further discussion'. Probably the commission ought to have been more explicit. But in a subsequent article in *The Tablet*, dated 8 January 1972, Bishop Butler takes the position that although the commission was silent on reservation and extraliturgical devotions, their teaching about the nature of Christ's presence in the sacrament provides an ample theological basis for these developments. 'There can be a time-lag,' he says, 'between realization of a doctrinal truth and development of consequent devotion and practice. A striking feature of Anglican history in this century has been first the recovery of a high doctrine of the eucharist, and secondly, but subsequently, the spread of the practice of reservation and the spread of devotion to the sacrament thus reserved.'

We now turn to the question of what kind of eucharistic theology is implied in reservation and in associated practices. It would certainly seem that such practices are most readily allied to a doctrine of the real abiding presence of Christ in the consecrated elements, though it must again be strongly emphasized that these elements are not to be considered in isolation, but always in the context of the believing and worshipping community. Belief in a real abiding presence may, however, find expression in a variety of theological formulations. On this question, as on others, a measure of theological pluriformity is permissible and even desirable.

Traditionally, in the West, belief in a real abiding eucharistic presence and the practices associated with such a belief have been supported by the doctrine of transubstantiation. However, I wish to show that this is by no means the only theological position compatible with such beliefs and practices. Protestants and Anglicans have been consistent in rejecting the doctrine of transubstantiation (and I have never subscribed to it myself) but it is historically important as the official eucharistic theology of the Roman Catholic Church and it remains today as part of Roman Catholic teaching even if it is no longer held to be explanatory. Likewise among the Eastern Orthodox a doctrine close to that of transubstantiation is held. Archbishop Athenagoras has made it clear that both in respect of eucharistic doctrine and in respect to the practice of reverential reservation the Orthodox are at one with

Rome,[13] even if devotion to Christ in the reserved sacrament has not been developed in the East as in the West.

It is important to recognize that the term 'transubstantiation' has borne several meanings during its history, and that some are more defensible than others. But the question is one of some complexity, and so I have deferred further discussion to a separate section at the end of this chapter. Meanwhile, I want to show that there are other theological formulations which are capable of sustaining a eucharistic theology and practice no less rich than what may be based on transubstantiation.

Today many theologians are likely to be attracted to the theology of transignification, as developed by P. Schoonenberg and other Dutch Catholic theologians in recent years. The philosophical background to their work is a modern one. Especially they utilize categories drawn from the writings of Husserl, Merleau-Ponty and Heidegger, that is to say, from representatives of phenomenology and existentialism. The ideas of importance for transignification are 'thing', 'reality' or 'thinghood', 'body', 'person', 'meaning', 'signification', 'sign', 'world' and 'worldhood'. Briefly, things are constituted ontologically in their thinghood or reality not by substance but by having a place in a world; a world, in turn, is not a mere aggregate of physical things, but a personally structured totality of meanings. Transignification is a change in the sign-reality of the bread and wine, which become 'for us' the body and blood of Christ. This is not a 'subjective' theory, though equally it does not suppose Christ's presence to be purely 'objective' – an inappropriate expression, in any case, for we are considering what goes on in the living context of the church. No doubt the theology of transignification, here sketched in the barest way, has its own inadequacies, but it does seem to be more adequate as well as more up-to-date than the theology of transubstantiation, and allows just as well for belief in a real abiding presence, conceived in a more definitely personal way.

There are also some theories of symbolism which seem to be compatible with belief in a real abiding presence in the eucharist. An illustration is afforded by the understanding of symbols developed by Paul Tillich in his theology. An important part of his view is that the symbol is no merely conventional sign attached to the reality it signifies, but does itself 'participate' in the reality. I doubt whether Tillich anywhere gives a very clear account of what he means by 'participation' but he does wish to indicate a relationship in which the symbol shares in the being of that which it symbolizes.

The various theological formulations I have mentioned (and others not mentioned) are not simply rivals. They are different approaches to interpreting the mystery of eucharistic presence. Admittedly, some are more adequate than others. Admittedly, too, there may be some extreme Protestant groups who completely deny Christ's eucharistic presence, and it is hard to see how such a view could in any way be reconciled to the Catholic view. But probably very few Christians go to that extreme. Among most, there is a belief in presence, sometimes more, sometimes less explicit, and hesitations about making it more explicit have sometimes arisen out of a legitimate critique of what has seemed the absolutizing of a particular theological formulation. The question to be addressed to Rome is: 'How far can the implicit belief in presence be accepted as bridging the gap between the different eucharistic theologies and practices?' But there would also be a question for some Protestants: 'How far has the critique of a particular formulation (transubstantiation) led to merely negative attitudes?'

Some Further Remarks on Transubstantiation

For a long time theologians have distinguished at least three fairly different ways of understanding the term 'transubstantiation'.[14] It is important that these differences be kept in mind in any discussion of the subject, especially since the meaning of 'transubstantiation' has come up again in the discussions between Roman Catholic and Anglican theologians.

1. We begin with the classic period in the history of transubstantiation. Although the expression had been used earlier

from time to time, it first received official sanction from the Lateran Council of 1215. Although the Council did not spell out the doctrine in detail, it did assert that *corpus et sanguis (Jesu Christi) in sacramento altaris sub speciebus panis et vini veraciter continentur, transsubstantiatis pane in corpus et vino in sanguinem potestate divina*.[15] This is a guarded statement, and preserves a good deal of mystery – the body and blood are 'contained' (*continentur*) under the 'phenomena' (*speciebus*) of bread and wine, and the transformation is wrought 'by divine power' (*divina potestate*). But what is the 'substance', implied in *transsubstantiatis*? It remained for St Thomas Aquinas to fill out the details in his well-known teaching. Most importantly, he understood 'substance' as a *metaphysical* term, and did not identify it with physical matter. Thus, the classic doctrine of transubstantiation, as formulated by Thomas, is actually a very austere one. He was sceptical of reports of eucharistic marvels in which the bread and wine were said to have been visibly converted into the body and blood of Christ.[16] His doctrine of transubstantiation ruled out the possibility of such marvels, for the change is metaphysical, not physical. The accidents (or phenomena) of bread and wine remain unchanged. Yet the terminology of 'substance' seemed to lend itself for the purpose of maintaining a doctrine of the eucharistic presence that would be realistic (and so in line with the strongly realistic teaching of many of the Fathers) without being materialistic. Thomas affirms a real presence, but he denies that such a presence as that of Christ in the eucharist could be visible even to the saints in heaven.[17] Thus, at least in its intention, the classic doctrine of transubstantiation is a rebuff to all crudely materialistic interpretations of Christ's sacramental presence, while at the same time it maintains that this is a real presence.

2. But as time went on, materialistic interpretations of transubstantiation prevailed more and more. This becomes clear if we set alongside the guarded statement of the Lateran Council, quoted above, some language from the Council of Constance, meeting almost exactly two centuries later. In the '*Interrogationes Wycliffitis et Hussitis proponendae*' we find the following: *Item, utrum credat, quod post consecrationem sacerdotis*

in sacramento altaris sub velamento panis et vini non sit panis materialis et vinum materiale, sed idem per omnia Christus. . .[18] It is clear that several major changes have taken place. We no longer have to do with a metaphysical change of substance, for substance has now been identified with physical matter, and the material bread and material wine have been done away and replaced by the body and blood of Christ. It is to be noted also that the word *species* (which I translated above as 'phenomen') has now disappeared, and instead we get the word *velamentum*, 'covering'. Instead of that which appears, we now have to deal with that which conceals; that is to say, the phenomena have now become 'mere appearances' in the sense of illusions which prevent us from seeing what is truly there. Significant too is the fact that *potestate divina* is no longer mentioned as the agency of the change, and the stress is laid instead on *post consecrationem sacerdotis*! We can only conclude that by the fifteenth century the once austere doctrine of transubstantiation had degenerated into the semi-magical teaching which the Reformers knew as transubstantiation and which they rejected, as in Article 28 of the *Book of Common Prayer*. They were right in rejecting this decadent form of the doctrine – this is a good example of the legitimate exercise of the Protestant principle *vis-à-vis* the Catholic substance – but it remains a question whether their polemic touches other ways of understanding transubstantiation, both earlier and later. However, the major defect of what I have called the 'decadent' form of transubstantiation was that by *abolishing* the material bread and wine, it really denied the sacramental and indeed the incarnational principle, according to which material realities, without ceasing to be material, become ontologically the presence of the divine. The connection with christology was seen by Bishop Gore when he wrote that 'transubstantiation in eucharistic doctrine is the analogue of nihilianism with regard to the incarnation'.[19] But unfortunately Gore, like the Reformers, seemed to have fastened only on the corrupt form of the doctrine.

3. When we pass on to the Council of Trent, we find the word 'transubstantiation' being used in a much broader way. To be sure, it still points to a real change or a substantial

76

change, but there is no attempt to spell this out too precisely. Edward Schillebeeckx remarks: 'At Trent, the word "transubstantiation" explained nothing, but simply stood for the Catholic as against the Protestant understanding of the eucharist.'[20] This seems an oversimplification, and there is in any case no one 'Protestant' way of understanding the eucharist. But we might agree that the word 'transubstantiation' has now come to stand for a view which asserts the real abiding presence of Christ in the eucharistic species, as against any view that denies this. In the decrees of the Council, we read: *Declarat Concilium per consecrationem panis et vini conversionem fieri totius substantiae panis in substantiam corporis Christi Domini nostri, et totius substantiae vini in substantiam sanguinis eius. Quae conversio convenienter et proprie a sancta catholica Ecclesia transsubstantiatio est appellata.* The canons similarly state: *quam quidem conversionem catholica Ecclesia aptissime transsubstantiationem appellat.*[21] Thus, while the word 'transubstantiation' continues to assert a real abiding presence of Christ in the eucharist, the precise 'how' of this presence is left unexplained and it is simply claimed that the word is one that may be suitably (*convenienter, proprie, aptissime*) used, and has been so used by the church. This, of course, was the contention of the Roman Catholic theologians who reached a measure of agreement on the eucharist with their Anglican interlocutors.

Critics of transubstantiation ought to be careful to interpret the doctrine in the best light, and not (as has usually been done) in the form which it took in the late Middle Ages. Yet, even when we do this, some difficulties remain. 1. If, as we are now being told, the word simply affirms a real presence without offering any explanatory model or theory, then it is a very misleading word for the purpose, since to all educated people the word 'transubstantiation' at once suggests a whole philosophical apparatus of categories – substance, accident, etc. 2. This philosophical apparatus is not one that readily commends itself today. 3. Words like 'substance' and 'transubstantiation' are (*pace* Trent) inappropriate because they are impersonal words and not suitable for indicating the presence of Christ among his people. It was from this circumstance that the doctrine of transubstantiation has historically had the effect of narrowly localizing the presence of Christ in the consecrated elements, rather than seeing these as the central vehicles or bearers of his presence in the context of the eucharistic community.

9

Quaestiones Disputatae:

3 Marriage

Marriage is another area of tension among the different churches, both in theology and practice. The Roman Catholic Church has held strictly to the view that marriage is indissoluble and it has therefore refused to countenance divorce and remarriage. Anglicans have tended towards a similarly strict view, but there are some variations among the different churches of the Anglican communion. The Orthodox, on the other hand, have permitted divorce and remarriage on a variety of grounds, and so have many of the Protestant bodies.

Distinctive of the Roman Catholic position is belief in a *vinculum* or bond, said to be metaphysical in character and to be indissoluble. Probably most Protestants reject the idea of such a bond, and have great difficulty even in understanding what such a metaphysical *vinculum* might be. They suspect that it is a semi-magical or semi-mythical idea, quite irrelevant to the empirical facts of married life. Nevertheless, I think that all Christians, Catholic and Protestant alike, are agreed that the Christian ideal of marriage is the lifelong monogamous union of the partners. So once again we have to ask whether there is some 'Catholic substance' that is assumed, explicitly or implicity, by all and in relation to which the various positions have to be understood.

Lady Oppenheimer has made the interesting point that (in at least some ways of understanding them) there is a parallel between the idea of a metaphysical *vinculum* in the theology of marriage and the idea of transubstantiation in the theology of the eucharist. Both ideas, she claims, teach that whatever the outward appearances may be, the true nature of things has been permanently changed by an inward meta-physical transformation. And she thinks that empirically minded people react so violently against such teaching that they go to the opposite extreme and miss what is true in it. 'The eucharist is reduced to a mere memorial service, marriage to a dissoluble contract. As long as the argument continues in these terms of reference, nothing but deadlock and prejudice come of it.'[1]

Let us agree that it must be very hard for a thoroughgoing empiricist, contemplating a broken marriage, to give credence to the words of Thomas Aquinas: 'Nothing supervenient to marriage can dissolve it; wherefore adultery does not make a marriage cease to be valid.'[2] He would have similar difficulty with Augustine: 'As long as they live, they are bound by the marriage tie which neither divorce nor union with another can destroy.'[3] Are we not dealing here with mere fictions?

But just as I have tried to show in the last chapter that the doctrine of transubstantiation teaches a truth which is capable of alternative (and perhaps even better) formulations and which corresponds to a widely held implicit belief in Christ's sacramental presence, so I think the idea of a *vinculum coniugale* may be alternatively formulated so as to preserve its essential truth – a truth which again is implicity recognized in the conviction that marriage *ought* to be a lifelong union and in the language of marriage services. But I think that the traditional way of talking about the *vinculum* has suffered from the same defect as traditional language about transubstantiation – it has been too impersonal. It has been framed in the metaphysics of substances and essences rather than in the ontology of personal being.

Like transubstantiation, the *vinculum* has been understood in different ways at different times, and there is a long complicated history to the concept. Since my own concern is to inquire into the validity of the concept and to try to restate whatever may be valid about it in more up-to-date and personalistic terms than were traditionally employed, I shall not say much about the history. In any case, the material is readily available elsewhere.[4] But there are a few points in this history that call for notice, because they will affect the subsequent discussion.

First, we may notice that the *vinculum* has sometimes been considered primarily as a moral bond (the expression *vinculum obligatorium* is quite common in Roman Catholic writers), but sometimes primarily as a metaphysical bond. According to E. Schillebeeckx, marriage was seen in the patristic age as 'a life commitment' which *ought* not to be dissolved; whereas in medieval times it was seen as an ontological union which *could* not be dissolved.[5] But he at once goes on to say: 'These two visions – the patristic view of marriage as a moral obligation and the scholastic view of marriage as an ontological bond – are not mutually exclusive, but rather mutually implicit. Both the patristic and the scholastic doctrines are firmly based on scripture.'[6]

I agree with Schillebeeckx that the moral and ontological aspects of the marriage bond mutually imply each other. Any moral obligation, considered in depth, reveals itself as having ontological foundations. Certainly, the solemn obligations undertaken in marriage cannot fail to affect the partners in the very depths of their being, that is to say, ontologically or metaphysically. Furthermore, we shall see that the marriage bond includes other deep-lying connections, besides moral obligation. So it was no distortion but a natural development when the patristic stress on obligation was expanded in the scholastic idea of an ontological bond.

Second, there were arguments over the question of the moment at which the marriage bond comes into being, or what it is that makes the marriage.[7] Is the bond formed by the solemn consent of the parties? Or is it formed by the consummation of their union in the sexual act? Again, this is a question which seems to call for an inclusive rather than an exclusive answer. The vows already form a bond, but that bond becomes fully a marriage bond and has indeed a new dimension added to it when the parties come together in the intimacy of sexual union. But as consummation came to be stressed rather than the vows, this led to a stressing of the ontological nature of the bond. The bond was understood in metaphysical and even mystical terms, for the union of husband and wife, according to scripture itself, is a figure of the union of Christ and the church (Eph. 5.25).

Third, we come to the sacramental understanding of marriage. Clearly, marriage is a natural institution, and Christian marriage has much in common with non-Christian marriage. But is there something more in Christian marriage, something that makes it distinctively sacramental? Historically, the question has sometimes been raised whether the indissoluble bond is found only where there is this 'something more', and the so-called 'Pauline privilege' (I Cor. 7.12–16) has been cited as evidence that non-Christian marriages are not indissoluble. The somewhat ambiguous Roman Catholic view is summed up in the sentence: 'Marriages contracted by pagans are indeed true marriages but are not considered so firm that they may not be dissolved in case of necessity.'[8] This is a point which we can only consider when we have ascertained more clearly what is the extra sacramental dimension said to be present in Christian marriage.

After these brief preliminary remarks on some of the topics that have been debated in the history of the subject, I shall now proceed to develop my own view of the matter, in the hope that it may provide some common ground between Catholic substance and Protestant principle. I shall argue that there is indeed a bond or *vinculum* which may properly be called ontological. It includes the strand of obligation, but there are other strands besides, among them an important one deriving from the nature of human sexuality. Moreover, I think this *vinculum* belongs to all marriage, Christian and non-Christian alike. The sacramental dimension of Christian marriage adds, as we shall see, something of the highest value and importance to natural marriage, but the *vinculum* is already there in natural marriage. This ontological *vinculum coniugale* is permanent, and so we shall finally have to ask about the practical consequences.

What then are the reasons for holding the view that has just been sketched out?

We begin with scripture. Marriage – and this applies to all marriage – is said to establish a relationship between the partners so close that it takes priority over blood relationships: 'They shall be one flesh' (Gen. 2.24). The word 'flesh' means here, as it often does in the Old Testament, the entire being of the human person.[9] To become 'one flesh' with the marriage partner is to become one in being with that person and so to undergo a profound ontological transformation. In the New Testament, the point is made even more forcibly. Jesus quotes the words about being 'one flesh' and adds: 'What therefore God has joined together, let not man put asunder' (Mark 10.9). The marriage bond is here seen as a work of God, and this is surely to ascribe it to a status that may fairly be called 'metaphysical' and that puts the bond beyond the range of what men can dispose or alter. But Jesus was not teaching anything new. He was simply reasserting the permanent ontological character of the marriage bond, as understood in the institution narrative of Genesis. What is new, however, is that he immediately goes on to dissociate his own teaching from the Old Testament laws permitting divorce – laws which by implication fail to measure up to the Old Testament understanding of marriage. Jesus forbids divorce and remarriage to his followers on the ground that they issue in adultery. This seems a very hard saying, and it is.

Presumably the word 'adultery' (*moicheia*), like the word 'fornication' (*porneia*), is not to be understood in some narrowly legal sense or only as a physical act. Elsewhere, indeed, Jesus condemns the undisciplined sexual desire as itself adulterous (Matt. 5.28). The words *moicheia* and *porneia* point to a misuse of sexuality as a consequence of which its effects are reversed. Instead of integrating persons, both in themselves and in the richer unity of 'one flesh', it becomes a disintegrating and disruptive force.

Consideration of this biblical evidence makes it very hard to disagree with Schillebeeckx that from it 'one conclusion and only one can be drawn: the bond of marriage cannot be dissolved by divorce'.[10]

I turn next to that strand in the marriage bond which arises from the pledging by the partners of themselves to each other in their solemn vows. What does it mean to take a lifelong vow?

The idea of permanent commitment is one that contemporary society finds foreign and distasteful. In his fascinating if also frightening book, *Future Shock*, Alvin Toffler describes contemporary America as the 'throw-away society'. Increasingly rapid change and mobility has brought increasing transience. Whereas people once held on as long as possible to their possessions and got as much out of them as possible, now rapidly changing fashions and the abundance of goods means that things like clothes, gadgets, automobiles and the like have a built-in obsolescence, for it is understood that they will be kept only a short time, then thrown away and replaced. Even the environmental crisis will not speedily change this habit of mind, for the economic system has for a long time been geared to it. But in a highly mobile society, the idea of transience has been extended to personal relations. In Toffler's chilling words, 'we have created the disposable person, the modular man'.[11] He applies this notion to marriage and suggests (whether seriously or with tongue in cheek, it is hard to tell) that in the future a person will normally have a series of marriage partners, each one suited to a different stage of life. (Whether there could be any equity as between men and women in such an arrangement is not discussed.) Another suggestion is that mobile business executives, realizing that high mobility may not be good for their wives and children, might swap wives and children with their colleagues as they move from one post to another.

We seem to be in a different world when we turn to Søren Kierkegaard's famous discussion of lifelong commitments in the three areas of friendship, vocation and marriage.[12] Are we to dismiss his views as perhaps a position that it was possible to hold in the nineteenth and earlier centuries, but impossible in the twentieth? We should remember that even in the nineteenth (or any other) century, the notion of lifelong commitment was not easy to accept. In marriage, for instance, two people commit themselves to each other 'for better or for worse'. This is to decide for a relationship that utterly transcends the moment in which the vows are made. In that moment, there can only be the faith that the relationship can be realized and sustained. Is it not madness to make such a decision? Would it not be more sensible and even more

84

humane to make a provisional commitment? If things turn out well, we carry on; if not, we try again with new partners. Is the twentieth century not wiser than earlier times in turning away from lifelong commitments?

To answer these questions, we have to consider what it means to be a person – or to become a person. One of the most obvious characteristics of a person, distinguishing him from an animal, is that he looks beyond the moment and pledges himself beyond the moment. All of us are continually, in small matters and in great, committing ourselves, making promises, taking on obligations. A human community depends for its continuing existence on the fidelity of its members to the commitments they have freely taken on themselves. A person, in turn, is shaped by his decisions and by the way he stands by them. They enter into his being and make him the person he is. In a person of any depth and integrity, we find that there is a core of abiding commitments that give to his whole life its set and character, making him a unified person rather than a bundle of loosely connected instincts, opinions, likes and dislikes, etc. The Christian faith itself is a good illustration of the kind of basic commitment I have in mind, but so is the marriage vow. Both of these may have times of stress, both call for constant renewal and deepening, both demand learning, growth and perseverance. Yet both are precious enhancements of the person who has entered into them, so that in the course of time he or she would be destroyed by their loss. Such commitments may properly be called 'ontological' and I think that some such commitments (not necessarily the two I have mentioned) are essential to the attainment of full personhood. Incidentally, I question whether the 'throw-away society' of modular friends and disposable wives is producing many persons of any depth.

My argument can be further strengthened by a brief consideration of human sexuality. This differs from sexuality in animals because it has become a personal relationship, involving much more than the physical and physiological aspects; or, to speak more accurately, it is in transition from being a physiological to becoming a fully personal relation. At its best, the sexual act is the most intimate and complete reciprocal self-giving of which two persons are capable, making them 'one flesh' in a new and liberating whole. And this is no *égoisme à deux*, for the marriage union is also the foundation of the family. Sexual union in consummated marriage (of course, I am not talking of only one act or even of the whole series of sexual acts in isolation from the context of daily companionship and sharing) profoundly and permanently affects the parties in the very core of their being, just as much as do the solemn vows. Through the psychophysical sexual relation, another strand is added to the ontological *vinculum*. A mutual belonging is established.

To be sure, human sexuality is never perfected. It is in constant danger of becoming a sinful depersonalized exploitation of the other for the sake of a physical gratification, and this can happen in marriage as well as outside of it. Yet because of the way the human being is constituted as a person (or as one having the potentiality for personhood), even promiscuous sexual acts, casually undertaken for the pleasure of the moment, seem to affect those who engage in them at a deeper level than they consciously realize. The personal dimension of human sexuality may be very much reduced, but it can hardly be altogether extirpated. It is in the light of this that we can understand Paul's assertion that even an act of intercourse with a prostitute forms a personal bond and makes 'one body' (I Cor. 6.16). Needless to say, this is not the marriage bond, for we have already seen that the *vinculum coniugale* has more strands to it than the sexual link in isolation. Nevertheless, it seems likely that even in a casual act the intimate union of the parties makes some permanent modification of each and forges some link between them. They are, after all, persons and not mere sex objects. But such acts do not build up the person but rather scatter personal being. Many such acts make it impossible for the one who has engaged in them to know the meaning of sexuality in its fully personal psychophysical character as in monogamous marriage, for he has already 'scattered' his personal being in a qualitative sense among so many others that he is no longer able to make that total act of self-giving which characterizes the sexual relation at its best and most intense.

A closely related point may be introduced here, one to which John R. Lucas has drawn attention in a discussion of the marriage bond.[13] It is the simple fact of the unalterability of the past. We may repent of what we have done, but we can never undo it or stay all its consequences. Even God 'cannot make what is past not to have been'.[14]

The bearing of this on what I have just been saying about the permanent effects of sexual union is obvious. The identity of each one of us is constituted by a history, including a sexual history. That history I must acknowledge as my own and, willy-nilly, it determines to a large extent what possibilities remain open to me today. I never begin *de novo* but always as one formed by a history. If that history already contains one or more sexual unions, and especially if it contains a union that has been solemnized in a previous marriage, then it profoundly affects and limits what I would be able to bring to a marriage today. It is no longer possible for me to give my whole self, for I am already tangled in bonds I cannot break. Even if in practice a second marriage turns out to be more fulfilling than a first one that has gone wrong, it cannot in the very nature of things have the potentialities of a first marriage – those that belong to personal total lifelong union. Thus, even if one were to agree that in certain circumstances the church might provide remarriage for divorced persons, it would seem that a different marriage service would have to be used, for the simple truth that what is done cannot be undone means that any subsequent marriage must be different in certain fundamental respects from a first marriage.

What I have said so far applies to the natural marriage bond. It remains to say something about the specific character of Christian marriage. We call such a marriage 'sacramental', and in it still another strand is woven into the bond. This is the strand of divine grace. It has become clear to us that marriage is no easy matter, to be undertaken lightly or unadvisedly. Is it not presumptuous for fallible human beings to take upon themselves lifelong vows? Is it not idealistic to talk of sexuality in the somewhat exalted terms I have been using when it is in fact such an unruly instinct? The Christian can only reply that he ventures to do and to say these things because he believes that God himself ratifies the marriage bond and strengthens those who have entered into the union. In becoming one flesh, the partners now constitute a Christian community, a tiny church, as it were, which, like the whole church, is the bride of Christ and the recipient of his faithful love.

This additional sacramental strand in the marriage bond may be compared to the permanent 'character' which, as some theologians believe, is conferred in the acts of baptism, confirmation and ordination. The marriage *vinculum* is in some respects different from such 'character', and this comparison must not be pushed too far, any more than the comparison with transubstantiation, made earlier on in the chapter.

The first conclusion to be drawn in this chapter is that whatever we may think of the antiquated terminology or the traditional arguments, an overwhelming case can be made out to show that the idea of a metaphysical *vinculum coniugale* does point to a reality – to a bond with several powerful strands, irreversibly affecting the parties in the depths of their beings and therefore to be reckoned ontological. No action taken by the parties themselves or by anyone else could finally annihilate that bond, though clearly it may be both weakened and flouted. To this extent then the Catholic substance is vindicated as the frame for any ecumenical discussion of marriage, and we can see it reflected implicity in the universal Christian acknowledgement that lifelong monogamous union is the ideal.

A second conclusion is that Christians must uphold the norm of lifelong union in marriage. The pressures of modern society are all against this and there is a temptation to the churches to change their marriage discipline to accommodate modern permissiveness. This would surely be a great mistake. I do not think that the Roman Catholic Church and any other churches which have practised a fairly strict marriage discipline would be helping contemporary society by compromising their position. Admittedly, there are many hard cases which call for compassion, but there are better ways of dealing with hard cases than abandoning the norm.

A third conclusion is that in a uniate relationship of the

churches different marriage disciplines might exist side by side. It is right that the Catholic substance should be upheld, but marriages after all do break down and the Protestant principle, where it permits remarriage, could be interpreted as a legitimate protest against a too rigorous application of the belief in indissolubility. Of course, although the Roman Catholic church has not countenanced divorce, it has recognized various grounds for annulling marriage, and at the present time some Roman Catholic moral theologians are exploring the reform and liberalizing of the concept of nullity so as to make the marriage discipline more compassionate. In such cases it is argued that the marriage has not taken place – some strand in the bond has been missing, some hidden impediment has been present, consummation (understood not merely in a physical way) has failed to come about. But clearly there are limits to what can be permitted along these lines, and there is the danger of stretching the idea of nullity to the point where it becomes an implausible fiction. So I would argue that some churches should make divorce available, and that this is not such a fundamental difference that it could not be accommodated within a uniate relationship. This could bring new problems, such as that of couples 'shopping around' for a soft discipline. But I think this would be outweighed by the fact that different disciplines, co-existing side by side yet without breaking essential Christian unity, are a far better witness to Christian freedom and a true diversity-in-unity than any compromise on a uniform practice could ever be. There are legitimate differences of opinion here, there is a genuine tension between the given ideal of marriage and the imperfect realization of that ideal in actual unions, there is finally the temptation to understand the norm in a narrowly legalistic way and therefore the legitimate protest against that legalism in the name of Christian freedom. Here again I see Catholic and Protestant views supplementing and correcting one another, but not susceptible of being combined in a dead-centre uniformity.

10

Quaestiones Disputatae:

4 Mariology

The place of Mary in faith and devotion is not so central as
the disputed questions we have considered so far, yet it is
bound to come up in discussions between Roman Catholics
and other Christians. We can begin by noting that there is
already a large area of agreement, and that Mary is honoured
among many Christians. Eastern Orthodox, Anglicans,
Lutherans, some Reformed, observe, to varying extents, the
festivals of the Blessed Virgin and accord her that reverence
that is fitting to her unique role in the economy of salvation.
All this, of course, is firmly based on what the New Testament tells us about her. The new interest in the feminine and
the belief that God has for too long been presented in exclusively masculine terms is also leading to a new awareness
of Mary and a willingness to reconsider her place in theology,
even among Protestant groups that have hitherto almost
ignored her.

Yet, when all this has been said, it must be admitted that
a considerable gulf still remains between Roman Catholics
and many other Christians in this matter. Roman Catholics
have in general gone much further than other Christians
(with the exception of the Orthodox) in devotion to Mary and
in developing a theology of Mary (mariology). In the words of
Vatican II, 'the church has endorsed many forms of piety
towards the Mother of God, provided that they were within
the limits of sound and orthodox doctrine'.[1] But just what are
'the limits of sound and orthodox doctrine'? The heart of
the difficulty is that Rome has worked out in considerable
detail and made *de fide* doctrines concerning Mary which, at

least *prima facie*, seem to go beyond what is warranted in scripture and in the most authentic tradition and which, in the view of some non-Romans, might even seem to threaten the unique place of Jesus Christ himself. There are two such doctrines in particular, both of which have been raised to the status of formal dogmas in recent times – the dogma of the Immaculate Conception, promulgated in 1854, and the dogma of the Assumption, promulgated in 1950. Of course, both of these dogmas had been believed for a much longer time, but the fact that they have now become dogmas and part of the official faith of the Roman Catholic Church has been seen by many people as a barrier in the way of continuing *rapprochement* between Rome and the separated churches.

In this chapter I shall try to deal with only one of these Marian dogmas – that which teaches her immaculate conception. I think it is the more difficult of the two. Clearly, it is not taught directly in scripture, and attempts to find indirect evidence for it in the Bible rest, I would say, on strained and implausible exegesis. Furthermore, the doctrine has had a stormy history. Bernard of Clairvaux rejected it, and so did many eminent medieval theologians, including Thomas Aquinas himself. The Eastern Orthodox, in spite of their veneration for Mary, reject this doctrine. Vladimir Lossky writes: 'The dogma of the Immaculate Conception is foreign to the Eastern tradition, which does not wish to separate the Holy Virgin from the sons of Adam . . . She was not holy in virtue of a privilege, of an exemption from the destiny common to all humanity, but because she has been kept from all taint of sin without any impairment of her liberty.'[2]

When one considers the weight of counter opinion, it is perhaps surprising that belief in the immaculate conception should have been made a dogma rather than remaining a pious opinion. It was the redoubtable Pius IX who took the step in 1854, and we may begin by listening to the words of the constitution *Ineffabilis Deus* in which the new dogma was promulgated: *Declaramus . . . beatissimam Virginem Mariam in primo instanti suae conceptionis fuisse singulari omnipotentis Dei gratia et privilegio, intuitu meritorum Christi Iesus Salvatoris humani generis, ab omni originalis culpae labe praeservatam*

91

immunem.[3] 'We declare . . . that the most blessed Virgin Mary in the first moment of her conception was, by the unique grace and privilege of God, in view of the merits of Jesus Christ the Saviour of the human race, preserved intact from all stain of original sin.' It was added that anyone dissenting from this belief should know that he 'had defected from the unity of the church' (*ab unitate Ecclesiae defecisse*).

Admittedly, this last polemical point would hardly be made today. But what does the non-Roman, whether Orthodox, Anglican or Protestant, say in the face of this dogma? Does it really constitute a major barrier in the way of drawing nearer to Rome? Or shall we find, as I hope we may have done in the cases of transubstantiation and the marriage *vinculum*, that what we have before us is a particular formulation, perhaps in unfortunate terminology, of something that does belong to the Catholic substance and which in some measure may already be implicitly acknowledged among those who are opposed to the particular formulation? Confronted with the dogma of Immaculate Conception, we have neither blindly to accept it nor angrily to reject it, but first of all to understand it. Then there will be the question whether the dogma or something close to it can be expressed in an alternative and more widely acceptable way. I believe myself that the trouble with immaculate conception is similar to the trouble we found with transubstantiation and with the notion of a metaphysical *vinculum* – namely, that the categories employed were too impersonal so that the Catholic substance was obscured and this in turn activated the Protestant principle of criticism.

Let us attend again therefore to the words of *Ineffabilis Deus*, quoted above. The sentence is heavily laden with implications and presuppositions of various kinds. It makes clear, for instance, that the doctrine of an immaculate conception of Mary is to be understood in the closest connection with other doctrines of the Christian faith – doctrines of incarnation, grace, redemption and also of man and sin. Now, this care to connect the doctrines is very important. Christian faith constitutes a whole and the several doctrines mutually imply and support each other. The meaning and truth of any particular doctrine is to be considered in the light of its coherence with other doctrines. This is especially the case with a peripheral doctrine, such as the one presently being considered. We have seen that there is no direct support for it in scripture and little in the tradition, so that its claims would have to be judged by considering whether it is entailed by other, more central doctrines.

But if we acknowledge the merit of *Ineffabilis Deus* for its effort to see Christian doctrine as a whole, we may nevertheless feel much less happy about the language used and the conceptuality which that language expresses. It is a language which, in some respects, seems very strange to us today. For example, the imagery of sin as 'stain' (*labe*) may well strike us as too impersonal; while the stress on Mary's being 'preserved' (*praeservatum*) from original sin may well seem far too negative, as does also the heavy emphasis on original sin which hangs like a cloud over the whole dogma.

Is it possible to find a new and different approach to the mystery of Mary's person – an approach that will continue to assert whatever belongs to catholic truth in the dogma of 1854 but one that will use more definitely personal and affirmative modes of expression? I think it is.

Let us begin by putting aside the understanding of sin as stain. The metaphor of sin as stain is indeed an ancient one, and almost universal among the races of mankind, but it belongs to a mentality which is no longer ours and which indeed was already out of date in 1854. To talk of sin as stain suggests that sin is something quasi-physical, and more than that, something that can exist in its own right in a Manichaean fashion. Let us substitute for that a more personal and more up-to-date way of understanding sin, namely, sin as alienation or estrangement. The sinner is alienated from God and consequently from his neighbour and even from himself. Original sin is that corporate alienation of the whole race from God that distorts human society.

But then we must go on and say that a life 'preserved' from original sin means a life not alienated, a life which has not been stunted and distorted by the alienation of the race. And it becomes at once clear that we are embarked upon what is not only a more personal but also a much more positive or affirmative way of understanding the truth of immaculate conception. To be free of sin or preserved from sin is to be close to God and to enjoy his grace.

Furthermore, although Western theologians have laid a heavy stress on the doctrine of original sin and although this doctrine was very much in the minds of the framers of *Ineffabilis Deus*, we must assert that equally there is an original righteousness and that grace as well as sin has been operating in the world since the creation. However deep the inroads of sin, the original righteousness of man created in the image of God has never been quite eliminated and the common grace of creation has never been quenched. A doctrine of total depravity has never been accepted by the mainstream of Christian theologians and, in any case, it would make nonsense of the Christian faith.

When God called Israel, when he made his covenants, when he gave a law and when he kindled a hope, could we say that he was concentrating in that people the righteousness and the grace that had not been destroyed by the fall? And could we say that, in the history of his people Israel, God was, so to speak, nursing that spark of righteousness that it might gain strength and burn more brightly and clearly. And could we say that with Mary the spark bursts into flame. She is the gathering up of the unscathed righteousness and the unquenched grace – she is 'full of grace' (Luke 1.28). It is a Catholic theologian, Ludwig Ott, who tells us that 'the essence of original sin consists (*formaliter*) in the lack of sanctifying grace'.[4] So what is negatively described as Mary's preservation from original sin means in an affirmative way her enjoyment of the divine grace. The moment had come when alienation was at an end, when mankind had been brought to the condition of being *capax Dei*, capable of receiving God in the gift of the incarnation.

Perhaps it needs to be added that in all this we are thinking of Mary not as a private individual with a private biography (though she was that) but as a public figure, in the sense that we are interested in her as a moment in the story of humanity or, better expressed, a moment in the history of God's dealing with humanity. Mary is part of a corporate history, and also part of salvation history. She is on the one hand in solidarity with Israel, and brings that history to its culmination. On the other hand, she is the first member of the new Israel, the Christian church, and already prefigures it. She is that point in humanity at which incarnation could take place.

One of the dangers that attend any theological reflection on Mary is that one may begin attributing to her what properly and uniquely belongs to Christ. One may invest so much in Mary that Christ begins to appear superfluous. It is then that the Protestant principle needs to operate in mariology, and Vatican II also warned against the dangers of exaggeration. Are we ourselves falling into this danger when, in an attempt to understand the meaning of immaculate conception, we attribute to Mary such an amplitude of righteousness and so distinctive an enjoyment of the divine grace? Are we already ascribing so much to her that it would no longer be Jesus Christ who brings the new humanity to light?

I do not think so. The official formulation of the dogma of Immaculate Conception made it clear that the gift and privilege which Mary enjoyed were hers 'in view of the merits of Jesus Christ the Saviour of the human race'. And again we have to remember the interlocking of Christian doctrines. The meaning of Mary is inseparable from and dependent on the meaning of Jesus Christ.

There is something more. I would say that the kind of righteousness we have seen reason to ascribe to Mary is of a different order from the righteousness that comes to expression in Christ himself. Mary's righteousness is continuous with the righteousness of Israel, it is the perfecting of the righteousness of the old dispensation. It is therefore essentially a receptive righteousness, making her, as we have said, *capax Dei*. She is ready to receive the divine gift. 'Be it unto me according to thy word' (Luke 1.38). The righteousness of Christ has also this character, especially in his obedience, but it has something more, something that we believe to be new in the history of mankind. The righteousness of Christ is a dynamic, creative, innovating righteousness, not to be contained within the category of a restored original righteousness. It points forward rather than back, it brings an eschatological promise. That is why in his case we cannot stop short of a doctrine of incarnation: the creative righteousness of God himself has in Christ come among men.

The difference between these two types of righteousness is underlined by the difference of sex. We must be careful not to exaggerate this point or to fall into stereotypes, and we have already seen that Christ's own righteousness had its passive, receptive side in obedience. But, generally speaking, the receptive type of righteousness finds expression in the feminine figure of Mary, just as Israel, the people among whom Mary's spiritual formation took place, is represented as the bride beloved of God. But the righteousness of the only begotten Son goes beyond the traditional righteousness and shares in the creativity of the Father.

Have we succeeded in building a bridge between the formal Roman Catholic dogma of the Immaculate Conception and that relatively unformulated understanding of Mary's person, drawn from scripture and from the implications of Christian doctrine, that has been characteristic of the Orthodox, many Anglicans and not a few Protestants? Only further discussion with Roman Catholic theologians could show whether the understanding of Mary's person outlined here contains all or most that would be considered essential to the dogma of 1854. Clearly, too, both this teaching and such devotional practices as might be connected with it would be explicit to different degrees in different non-Roman churches, though it could scarcely be completely absent anywhere if it is indeed so closely tied in with some central doctrines of the faith. But these are surely differences of belief and practice that are possible and desirable within a structure of unity with freedom. Though they may express themselves differently, many who are not Roman Catholics recognize the truth in the words: 'Blessed be her immaculate conception!'

I I

Quaestiones Disputatae:

5 Authority

I have left to the last the most difficult of all the disputed questions – authority. The coming together of the divided churches into a new unity with diversity will demand an intricate adjustment between the need for some cohesive authority and the legitimate Christian exercise of freedom and autonomy.

On the whole, authority tends to go with the Catholic substance and freedom with the Protestant principle, yet this is too simple a view of the matter and we find the conflict of authority and freedom in Protestant churches too.

The Catholic emphasis on the given, on tradition, on a continuity between the existing church and Christ himself, tends to invest the church with a high degree of authority. Until very recently and even in considerable measure today, there is an authoritarianism in the Roman Catholic Church, and those accustomed to less rigid structures find it hard to come to terms with this. The priest in his parish, the bishop in his diocese, above all, the Pope in the church as a whole, seem to exercise an authority which is foreign to the mentality of most Protestants and Anglicans. Perhaps for two hundred years or so after the Reformation the Protestant pastor was just as much an authority figure in his parish as the Catholic priest, but the gradual secularization of Protestant countries has eroded that authority and few today would want to see it restored.

The very notion of a Protestant principle of criticism, questioning and reform means a relativizing of all authority other than that of God himself. Even the word of God, the

Bible, which for a time enjoyed an absolute authority among Protestants, has been relativized by biblical criticism. But if the Roman Catholic Church seems far too authoritarian in Protestant eyes, the liberal Protestant denominations must seem far too permissive to Catholic observers. Sometimes theologians teach far out doctrines and are allowed to continue to teach students for the ministry. Marriage discipline is sometimes relaxed to conform to the *mores* of the permissive society. Catholics who are accustomed to having clear instruction in faith and conduct must think Protestant churches hopelessly confused or even in a state of disintegration.

We should recognize, of course, that there may be many reasons for Protestant permissiveness. On the question of tolerating very unorthodox teaching, for instance, one may agree that sometimes this toleration arises simply from indifference. But at its best, it arises from the belief that the best answer to deviant beliefs is not to try to suppress them but to bring them out into the open and, by free criticism, to show what is mistaken in them as well as learning something of the truth that is hidden in every error. No doubt there is a risk in such permissiveness, but it is a risk worth taking if there is to be progress in theological understanding. Furthermore, it could be argued that willingness to take this risk is so far from evincing indifference that it rather shows a fundamental confidence in Christian truth and in the capacity of this truth to stand on its own feet and survive in the free give and take of intellectual debate. One may recall the words of Irenaeus about the eroneous teachers of his day: *Adversus eos victoria est sententiae eorum manifestatio*[1] – 'The best way to beat them is to let people clearly understand what they are saying.' Protestants and Anglicans would need to take a long hard look at any move towards closer relations with Rome if there was any danger that it might impair their reasonable liberties.

However, there has been movement on both sides. Rome has abandoned some of the old rigidity, though one feels that there is still quite a way to go towards a broader freedom. On the other side, Protestants (or some of them) are coming to have a better understanding of the teaching office of the church and of the role of the church as the interpreter of scripture. This has come about above all through discussions between Catholic and Protestant groups on what was once the very divisive question of scripture and tradition. These are no longer seen as rivals but as complementing one another.

Even when we come to the central symbol of authority in Roman Catholicism, the papacy, the position is by no means as hopeless as it must once have seemed. In the first place, the prestige of the papacy has been greatly enhanced in recent years, far beyond the bounds of the Roman Catholic Church itself. John XXIII, by his warm loving spirit, and then Paul VI, with his manifest concern for peace and for the wretched of the earth, have won respect for themselves and for their office not only among non-Catholics but also among non-Christians. In the second place, the new emphasis on collegiality in Roman Catholic theology, though its full implications are not yet clear, does move in the direction of qualifying the autocratic character of the papacy and so of reducing the force of some of the traditional objections.

Clearly, we are still far from a solution of the problem, but I believe that many Protestants and Anglicans accept that the papacy will have an important part to play in the future of the whole church, and not least in the promotion of Christian unity. Certainly, the papacy could not be abolished as the price of unity; the effect would be the opposite from what was desired. I do not think either that the Pope should be reduced to a mere figurehead or ceremonial president. The papacy can and, we must hope, will provide dynamic leadership for the whole Christian church. But such leadership can come only from a papacy truly integrated with the bishops and eventually with the whole people of God. The Pope is a sacramental person, an embodiment of the whole church, but he is nothing apart from the church. Whether a renewed and renewing papacy can do what we hope from it remains to be seen, and it will be understood that I am talking of the long term – it may take two centuries or more to come to that point.

For there is one formidable obstacle still in the way, and I have not yet mentioned it. I mean infallibility. I must frankly acknowledge that I do not see any way in which this doctrine

99

could ever become acceptable to Anglicans and Protestants. Even if, through a development of the idea of collegiality, one were to see infallibility as belonging to the church as a whole, the idea would still be inacceptable. For, as I understand it, the doctrine of infallibility means that, given certain carefully specified conditions, then on a particular occasion and on a particular matter one can assert that the Pope (or the church) has made a pronouncement that is guaranteed to be free from error. This, as it seems to me, is not something one can believe either about the people of God *in via* or about their human leaders. One may have great respect for the utterances of Popes and, among the Orthodox, Anglicans and Protestants, there would be still more respect for the utterances of an ecumencial council of the church. But the possibility of error is not excluded, for no human agency is guaranteed against error. The Anglican attitude towards councils is stated thus by Henry Chadwick: '1. While they are important, their definitions never quite possess a final and absolute authority in such a sense that they may not need supplementation or even correction by later councils with wiser, second thoughts; 2. their decisions do not make it superfluous to study scripture and to use one's reason.'[2] These remarks would, of course, apply *a fortiori* to any papal pronouncements.

With great courage, Hans Küng has written: 'We should like to substitute for the term "infallibility" the term "indefectibility".'[3] We should be clear, however, that this is not just substituting one term for another, but abandoning one concept for another. By 'indefectibility' is meant the persistence of the church in truth, the fact that it is constantly recalled to truth from whatever errors may have overtaken it. It has this indefectibility because the truth of Jesus Christ persists in it and finally because God himself has called it into being for his own purposes. The indefectibility of the church is really a corollary of belief in God. We could all come together on indefectibility, but infallibility, in the narrower sense, remains a barrier.

Need it, however, be a barrier to the kind of uniate relationship we have been advocating in this book? Such a relation assumes a measure of autonomy in the participating ecclesial bodies. Since Rome is the centre, then all these participating churches would in some sense acknowledge the primacy of the bishop of Rome, but it could well be the case that the degree of his authority would be different in different parts of the united church.

In these last few chapters we have been exploring some of the possibilities for coming together in disputed areas. But have we fallen into the error, mentioned at an earlier stage, of becoming too introspective and concentrating so much on the life of the church that we have forgotten the larger life of mankind. In our final chapter, we shall redress the balance by looking outward once more.

12

The Wider Ecumenism: Christianity and Other Faiths

Christianity is one faith among many in the world today. Some of these other faiths are secular; for instance, Marxism. Others are religious, and some of them are older than Christianity itself, such as Buddhism and Hinduism. By a religious faith, as distinct from a secular faith, I mean one that inculcates an attitude to the holy or transcendent, and I believe with Robert Schlette in his splendid study of religions that human salvation requires not only morality but 'a genuinely responsible attitude in relation to what may be described quite generally as the transcendent mystery'.[1] What then is to be the relation of Christianity to these other great religious faiths?

This relation has been a variable one in the past. Christianity itself began as a persecuted sect, but the time was to come when it turned persecutor. When there was no persecution, nevertheless there often lingered an incredibly negative attitude towards non-Christian faiths. They were to be swept away by evangelism and education, and everyone was to be brought into the Christian fold. But just as the ecumenical spirit within Christianity has transformed the relations of the various churches and denominations, so there is a new spirit of understanding *vis-à-vis* the non-Christian religions. Yet this needs to be carefully studied. From attitudes of Christian superiority it is easy to go to the opposite extreme and to say that all religions are equally good or equally true. The easy-going tolerance that can assent to any and every point of view is no help, and is in fact not much different from the scepticism that would dismiss all religious faith as illusion. Both are non-committal, but the core of religious faith consists precisely in commitment. Because we are finite beings, that commitment comes for each person in a particular situation and in a particular stream of history. Thus, while we must avoid letting the commitment of religion become a narrow fanaticism, we must equally struggle against letting it become so generalized that anything worthy of being called a faith commitment has been eliminated and our attitude to religion ends up as one of indifference or mild benevolence.

The relation between Christianity and other faiths is to be seen in dialectical terms. The Greeks spoke of the *tonos* or tension of the well-functioning bow, and we have to consider the tension between the particular commitment of the Christian and his openness to other faiths.

I do not think it is going too far to say that the beginnings of this tension go back to the New Testament. Difficult questions of exegesis arise here, but we find expression, sometimes in the same writer, both of the particular Christian commitment and of the recognition that God has not withheld the knowledge of himself from the great mass of mankind. The synoptic gospels, explicitly or implicitly, stress the unique authority of Jesus, but they could hardly be said to make an *exclusive* claim. The fourth gospel speaks of the Logos that has been in the world since the beginning and that in some sense lightens every man, but it speaks also of the 'only begotten' Son and declares that no one comes to the Father except through him. In Acts, Peter is represented as saying that there is salvation in no one except Christ, but in the same book Paul finds some common ground between the Christian gospel and the faith of the Athenians. It has been vigorously disputed whether the early chapters of Paul's own epistle to the Romans recognize some kind of natural theology – and perhaps the rival exegeses have been not a little influenced by the theological preferences of the exegetes. The writer to the Hebrews certainly thinks of Jesus as the author and finisher of our faith, yet the history of faith is traced back not only to the Hebrew patriarchs but to Noah and other mythical figures who belong to the whole human race. John Baillie, in a criticism of Barth's exclusive christocentrism, claims that this passage in Hebrews shows us 'the earliest Christian way of recognizing and explaining the common elements that pervade all the religions and therefore all the moral traditions of mankind'.[2]

When we turn from the scriptures to the history of the church's teaching, it can be affirmed that *on the whole* the church has not claimed that it exclusively enjoys a genuine knowledge of God. The Roman Catholic Church has recognized a true knowledge of God in the non-Christian religions and in philosophy. Anglican theology has taken a similar view, and so has liberal Protestantism in such notable representatives as Schleiermacher and Troeltsch. But it must be conceded that from the early days onward there has always been a counter-current to this mainstream of the church's thinking, and it acquired new force at the time of the Reformation. In our own time, this counter-current has flowed powerfully indeed, in the theology of Karl Barth and those who have been influenced by him. However, the great and deserved influence of Barth and his followers should not blind us to the fact that their claim that the knowledge of God is to be found exclusively in the Christian gospel is really a deviation – and, in my opinion, a very unfortunate one – from the mainstream teaching of the church throughout the greater part of its history.

When we pass from scripture and tradition to questions of evidence and common sense, the case against any belief in one unique exclusive revelation becomes overwhelming. Most of this evidence has accumulated only during the past hundred years or so, but Christians have been slow to adjust to it or to face its more radical implications. The evidence was perhaps more familiar to students of fifty years ago in the great days of liberal theology than it is now, and the very subjects on which it is based have been sadly neglected in theological faculties and colleges in recent times, though they have been revived in departments of religious studies. The evidence may be briefly summarized under three headings.

1 The findings of anthropology

Beginning with the work of such pioneers as E. B. Taylor, investigators have more and more laid bare the origins and earliest stages of religion, and have shown how even the most advanced religious beliefs and practices have not suddenly descended from heaven but can be traced back to very humble beginnings. Scholars such as Robertson Smith showed how biblical religion itself has roots in the common matrix of beliefs and practices shared by all the Semitic peoples. Naturally enough, those who had been taught that the revealed word of the Bible is *toto caelo* different from the idolatrous projections of 'heathenism' felt their security threatened. They often reacted by trying to suppress the new ideas, as actually happened in the case of Robertson Smith, who was dismissed from his teaching duties at Aberdeen in 1881. But inevitably the new teaching won acceptance, and today we see the whole religious experience of mankind, certainly as very richly differentiated, yet also as having threads of continuity.

2 *The science of comparative religion.*

In the later part of the nineteenth century, the researches of such scholars as Friedrich Max Müller opened up to the Western mind on a larger scale than ever before the vast spiritual treasures of the Eastern religions. It became possible to see Christianity not as an isolated phenomenon but as one of several classic ways in which the holy has spoken to men and become known. Sometimes we come across rather pathetic attempts to isolate the *differentia* of Christianity, to say what is unique in it and shared by no other religion. Every religion has its own distinctiveness and its own peculiar symbols, but the comparative study of religions has brought to light a great deal that they have in common. Also, many of the differences (as between, for instance, a mystical and a prophetic type of religion) are differences that recur within all faiths rather than differences that separate one faith from another.

3 *Expanded world outlook.*

This began with Copernicus, but it has been in recent times and especially now in the age of space exploration that we have become increasingly aware that our earth and its history have only an infinitesimal place in the vast setting of the cosmos. The overwhelming probability is that there are and have been and will be in the universe countless billions of histories having some similarity to the history that goes on here on earth. Empirical proof of this will possibly come before long as we extend our observations into space and time, but for the present it may be taken as a high probability. This must give us pause in claiming for any event in our history that it is the once-for-all exclusive revelation of God.

John Baillie quotes an enthusiastic Barthian as saying: 'Whosoever recognizes other sources of revelation besides Christ does not belong to the Christian Church.' Baillie rightly adds that we need not be unduly worried by this excommunication.[3] But it is more disturbing to find so eminent a theologian as Emil Brunner writing: 'A real Christian faith is impossible apart from the conviction that here and *here alone* is salvation.'[4] To put it bluntly, this is fanatical talk.

To the considerations already mentioned, it should be added that at the present time there are compelling practical reasons that call for a new and genuine openness on the part of Christianity towards other faiths. One such practical reason is that within our constantly shrinking world, the encounter of faiths, already begun, will become more and more critical. Paul Tillich has remarked: 'A theology which is not able to enter into a creative dialogue with the theological thought of other religions misses a world-historical occasion and remains provincial.'[5] In passing, however, it may be asked whether Tillich himself was really able to engage in what he calls 'creative dialogue', for his teaching that in the non-Christian religions we find 'preparatory' revelation as contrasted with the 'final' revelation of Christianity hardly allows for that openness which is the precondition of true dialogue. Another practical consideration is that all religions today are threatened by the rising tide of secularism in its many forms. It may be sad that people are willing to co-operate only when driven to it by a common danger, but it may be the possibility of seeing mankind engulfed by a brutal materialism that will bring to the world religions the realization of how much they have in common and will eventually lead to some significant measure of co-operation among them.

Yet, in spite of all the factors that count against it, the isolationist view is still strong in the Christian churches. Admittedly, responsible theologians no longer talk in the crudely offensive terms that were common in the past. But subtler ways of denigrating the religions are employed. Some of the followers of Barth, including those who have given a secular twist to his theology and who are more anxious to ally themselves with secular ideologies such as Marxism than with the non-Christian religions, engage in the criticism of all religion, including the Christian religion, as human fabrications. They tell us that all these religions, including the Christian religion, are judged and condemned by the Christian revelation, which is said to be essentially different from religion and the end of religion. But the distinction between religion and revelation is not possible in the form assumed here. It would surely be the height of arrogance to deny that there is genuine God-given revelation in other religions besides Christianity and to assert that these religions are merely works of man.

There can be creative dialogue among the great religions only if they can meet in a spirit of openness. This cannot happen if Christians are unwilling to credit other faiths with being the recipients of divine revelation or if they cherish the somewhat imperialistic aim of converting all people to the Christian faith. To give up that aim does not mean the end of mission, but it does mean that mission has to be rethought.

Let it be said, however, that while advocating open dialogue, I am very far from recommending any kind of syncretism, if by this is meant a merging of the best elements from the religious traditions in a new synthesis. It is true that there have always been a few people to whom a syncretistic ideal of religion has made a strong appeal. The Roman emperor Alexander Severus is said to have had busts of Orpheus, Abraham, Apollonius of Tyana and Jesus Christ in his oratory. The Renaissance scholar Pico della Mirandola is another noted example of the syncretistic mind and there have been a number of modern movements with similar tendencies. But the attempt to mix religious traditions is like the attempt to mix styles of art. It results in something rootless, inauthentic and often superficial and sentimental.

Even worse, perhaps, is the attempt, sometimes made by religiously inclined philosophers, to distil in the form of a metaphysic or world view the universal truths that are supposed to underlie all religions, and then to offer this metaphysic as a surrogate for faith. The abstract results of such speculations may have some appeal for academic minds that have never had much exposure to the world, but they can never have the power of living religions with their concrete if untidy symbolisms.

If then we reject both isolationism and syncretism, we are driven to look for that dialectical (or dialogical) tension which I likened to the *tonos* of the well-constructed and well functioning bow. It is the tension between the ultimate commitment to a living religious faith and the openness to the truths of other faiths.

It is here that the parallel with the ecumenical movement begins to appear, so that we can rightly speak of a wider ecumenism as between Christianity and the world religions. In the past, the divided churches of Christendom have shown in their dealings with each other much of the fanaticism that has characterized relations between hostile religions. Christians have unchurched other Christians, burned them and made every effort to stamp them out of existence. All that, we hope, has long ago been left behind, and today we see great efforts among the churches to draw together. On the ecumenical scene, the most promising efforts are those that respect genuine diversity and aim not at a drab uniformity but at a type of relationship which will maximize both unity and diversity.

This points to a possible relation among the great religions of the world. It would be a relation in which there is no foolish attempt to mix traditions, still less to eliminate all traditions except one, but a relation in which each can be loyal to his own tradition while holding himself open to others. Perhaps the idea has been best expressed by W. E.

Hocking in his teaching about 'reconception'.[6] As religions get to know each other, they begin to reconceive themselves in the light of what they learn from the other faith. This takes place without people moving out of one religion into another. In India, for example, Hinduism has been gradually forsaking its former indifference to social conditions under the influence first of Islam and then of Christianity. At first the interest in bettering social conditions expressed itself only in heterodox reforming groups, but it is now becoming part of mainstream Hinduism.

What then does this mean for mission, to come back to our earlier question? Not that it should be abolished, but that its true purpose must always be kept in view. That purpose is the bringing of more abundant life, the spread of love and truth. This has always been the true purpose of Christian mission, but it has sometimes been obscured, and more attention has been paid to making converts and increasing the membership of the church. It may well be that love and truth can grow, and life become more abundant, within the religion of those to whom the mission is directed. Furthermore, every genuine mission that seeks to bring truth and love must be prepared to receive mission. It must be prepared for reconception in its own thinking as well as seeking to induce it in the thinking of others.

The nineteenth-century ideal of the conversion of all nations to the Christian religion, preferably in its Western and Protestant form, is a thing of the past. As far as we can see, there will be religious pluralism on this planet and that is probably a good and healthy state of affairs, if we can have such pluralism without animosities or destructive rivalries. This is a time when, in the confrontation of races, nations and ideologies, not only the Christian church but all the religions of the world have an opportunity to lead men into a genuine humanity and away from the dangers that beset them. Finally, it is the unity of mankind, not just of the church, that is our goal, but a true unity with freedom, such as the church knows in its own life.

Notes

Chapter 1

1. Rudolf Bultmann, 'The Christological Confession of the World Council of Churches', *Essays Philosophical and Theological*, SCM Press 1955, pp. 273–90.
2. Don Cupitt, 'One Jesus, Many Christs?', *Christ, Faith and History*, ed. S. W. Sykes and J. P. Clayton, CUP 1972, pp. 131–44.
3. Maurice Wiles, *The Remaking of Christian Doctrine*, SCM Press 1974, p. 10.
4. Rudolf Schnackenburg, *The Church in the New Testament*, Search Press, London and Herder & Herder, NY 1965, p. 118.
5. George H. Tavard, *Two Centuries of Ecumenism*, New American Library, NY 1962, p. 18.

Chapter 2

1. Jacques Maritain, *Integral Humanism*, Scribners, NY 1968, pp. 165–6.
2. William James, *A Pluralistic Universe*, Longmans 1909, pp. 321–2.
3. William James, *The Varieties of Religious Experience*, Longmans 1952, p. 27.
4. Gordon D. Kaufman, *Systematic Theology*, Scribners, NY 1968, p. 58.
5. Stephen W. Sykes, *Christian Theology Today*, Mowbrays 1971, p. 33.
6. K. S. Latourette, *A History of Christianity*, Eyre & Spottiswoode, London and Harper & Row, NY 1953, p. 515.
7. Ian Henderson, *Power without Glory*, Hutchinson, London and John Knox Press, Atlanta 1969, p. 6.

8. Alexander Solzhenitsyn, *August 1914*, The Bodley Head 1972.

9. Bryan R. Wilson, 'Religion in a Secular Society', *Sociology of Religion*, ed. R. Robertson, Penguin Books 1969, p. 156.

10. Paul Tillich, *Systematic Theology*, James Nisbet 1968 and University of Chicago Press 1967, vol. III, pp. 169–70.

Chapter 3

1. R. H. Thouless, *An Introduction to the Psychology of Religion*, CUP 1950, pp. 51–2.

2. Reinhold Niebuhr, *The Nature and Destiny of Man*, James Nisbet 1943, vol. II, p. 320, and Scribners, NY 1949.

3. Cardinal Augustin Bea, *Unity in Freedom*, Harper & Row 1964, p. 214.

4. Ray L. Hart, *Unfinished Man and the Imagination*, Herder & Herder, NY 1968, p. 26.

5. D. M. MacKinnon, *The Stripping of the Altars*, Collins 1969, p. 81.

Chapter 4

1. Karl Rahner, 'Some Problems in Ecumenism Today' (mimeographed lecture), pp. 1–2 and 6.

2. Karl Rahner, *The Christian of the Future*, Search Press, London and Herder & Herder, NY 1967, p. 34.

3. Karl Rahner, *The Church after the Council*, Herder & Herder, NY 1966, p. 25.

4. Jürgen Moltmann, *The Crucified God*, SCM Press, London and Harper & Row, NY 1974, p. 277.

5. Ian Henderson, op. cit., p. 101.

6. Hans Küng, *The Church*, Burns & Oates, London and Sheed & Ward, NY 1967, p. 355.

7. Paul Tillich, op. cit., vol. III, p. 245.

8. The English Hymnal, No. 390.

Chapter 5

1. Rudolf Bultmann, *The Gospel of John: A Commentary*, Blackwells, Oxford and Westminster Press, Philadelphia 1971, pp. 512-13.

2. Cyprian, *On the Unity of the Catholic Church*, viii.

3. Douglas R. Jones, *Instrument of Peace*, Hodder & Stoughton 1965, p. 114.

Chapter 6

1. J. G. Davies, *Every Day God*, SCM Press 1973, p. 278.
2. John Knox, 'A Plea for a Wider Ecumenism', *Realistic Reflections on Church Union*, ed. John Macquarrie, Argus-Greenwood Press 1967, p. 27.
3. George H. Tavard, 'Consultations on Church Union: A Catholic Perspective', USCC Publications 1970, pp. 30ff.
4. John Knox, art. cit.
5. Ian Henderson, op. cit., p. 81.
6. John Macquarrie, 'What Still Separates Us from the Catholic Church? An Anglican Reply,' *Concilium*, vol. IV, 1970, p. 45.
7. Georges Florovsky, *Bible, Church, Tradition: An Eastern Orthodox View*, Nordland Publishing, Belmont 1972, pp. 39–40.
8. Edward P. Echlin, 'Unity without Absorption', *Journal of Ecumenical Studies*, vol. IX, 1972, pp. 51–2.
9. Cardinal Jan Willebrands, 'Moving towards a Typology of Churches', *The Catholic Mind*, 1970, p. 40.

Chapter 7

1. *The Apostolic Ministry*, ed. K. E. Kirk, Morehouse-Barlow, NY 1946, p.v.
2. R. C. Moberly, *Ministerial Priesthood*, John Murray 1910, p. 254.
3. *The Documents of Vatican II*, ed. W. M. Abbott, Geoffrey Chapman, London and Herder & Herder, NY 1966, p. 534.
4. *A New Catechism*, Herder and Herder, NY 1967, p. 360
5. R. C. Moberly, op. cit., p. 243.
6. 'The Ordained Ministry in Ecumenical Perspective', *Study Encounter*, vol. VIII, 1972, p. 21.
7. in *Realistic Reflections on Church Union*, pp. 37ff.

Chapter 8

1. Cf. *Modern Eucharistic Agreement*, ed. A. C. Clark and H. R. McAdoo, SPCK 1973.

2. Justin, *Apology*, I, lxv.

3. Tertullian, *Ad uxorem*, II, 5.

4. Gregory Dix, *A Detection of Aumbries*, Dacre Press 1942, pp. 7–8.

5. Ibid., pp. 18–19.

6. A. A. King, *Eucharistic Reservation in the Western Church*, Mowbrays 1965, pp. 9–11.

7. M. Moreton, in an unpublished paper to which I am much indebted.

8. *Apostolic Tradition*, xxxvii.

9. S. P. J. van Dijk and J. H. Walker, *The Myth of the Aumbry*, 1957, p. 79f.

10. E. Schillebeeckx, *The Eucharist*, Sheed & Ward 1968, p. 144.

11. Maurice Wiles, *The Making of Christian Doctrine*, CUP 1967, p. 119.

12. J. Jungmann, *Miss. Soll.*, IV, ii, 13.

13. in *The Tablet* of 8 January 1972.

14. Cf. F. H. Hall, *Dogmatic Theology*, Longmans 1921, vol. IX, pp. 126 ff.

15. H. Denzinger, *Enchiridion Symbolorum*, Herder & Herder 1957, 430.

16. Cf. J. Powers, *Eucharistic Theology*, Burns & Oates 1968, p. 110.

17. *S. Th.*, III, q. 76, a. 8.

18. H. Denzinger, op. cit., 666.

19. C. Gore, *Dissertations*, John Murray 1895, p. 283.

20. E. Schillebeeckx, op. cit., p. 41.

21. H. Denzinger, op. cit., 877 and 884.

Chapter 9

1. Helen Oppenheimer, 'Is there an Indissoluble Metaphysical *Vinculum*?', *Theology*, May 1975.

2. *S. Th.*, III (supp.), 62, 5.

3. *De Nup. et Concup.*, i, 10 (quoted by St Thomas ad loc.).

4. Cf. G. H. Joyce, *Christian Marriage: An Historical and Doctrinal Study*, Sheed & Ward 1948.

5. E. Schillebeeckx, *Marriage: Secular Reality and Saving Mystery*, Sheed & Ward 1965, vol, I, p. 203.

6. Ibid., p. 204.

7. Cf. Terence B. Cunningham, 'The Bond of Marriage', *The Meaning of Christian Marriage*, ed. E. McDonagh, Gill & Son 1963, p. 94.

8. Art. cit., p. 96.

9. Kenneth Grayston, 'Flesh', *A Theological Wordbook of the Bible*, ed. Alan Richardson, SCM Press, London and Macmillan Co., NY 1950, p. 83.

10. E. Schillebeeckx, op. cit., vol. I, p. 207.

11. Alvin Toffler, *Future Shock*, Bantam Books 1970, p. 97.

12. In *Either/Or*, Princeton University Press 1972.

13. John R. Lucas, 'Notes on the Doctrine of a Metaphysical *Vinculum*', *Theology*, May 1975.

14. St Thomas, quoted by Lucas ad loc.

Chapter 10

1. *The Documents of Vatican II*, p. 94.

2. Vladimir Lossky, *The Mystical Theology of the Eastern Church*, James Clarke 1957, p. 140f.

3. H. Denzinger, op. cit., 1641.

4. Ludwig Ott, *Fundamentals of Catholic Dogma*, Mercier Press 1958, p. 199.

Chapter 11

1. Irenaeus, *Adv. Haer.*, I, xxxi, 4.

2. Henry Chadwick, 'The Status of Ecumenical Councils in Anglican Thought', *Orient. Christ. Analecta*, No. 195, 1973, p. 407.

3. Hans Küng, *Infallible?*, Collins 1971, p. 150.

Chapter 12

1. H. R. Schlette, *Toward a Theology of Religions*, Search Press, London and Herder & Herder, NY 1966, p. 15.

2. John Baillie, *The Sense of the Presence of God*, OUP 1962, p. 133.
3. John Baillie, *Our Knowledge of God*, OUP 1939, p. 18.
4. Emil Brunner, *The Mediator*, Lutterworth Press 1934, p. 201.
5. Paul Tillich, op. cit., vol. III, p. 6.
6. W. E. Hocking, *Living Religions and a World Faith*, Allen & Unwin 1940, pp. 190ff.

Index of Names